Other books by William Barrett

THE TRUANTS
ILLUSION OF TECHNIQUE
IRRATIONAL MAN

DEATH OF THE SOUL

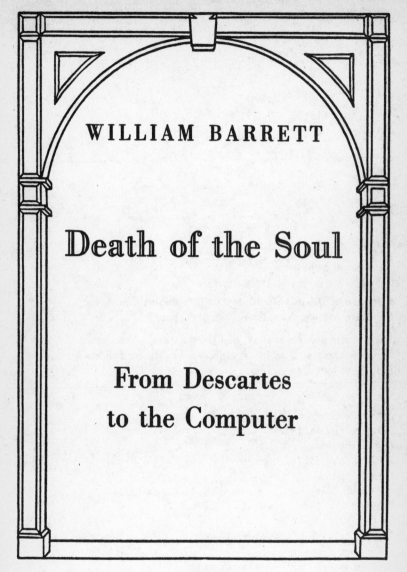

WILLIAM BARRETT

Death of the Soul

From Descartes
to the Computer

ANCHOR BOOKS
DOUBLEDAY
NEW YORK LONDON TORONTO SYDNEY AUCKLAND

An Anchor Book
PUBLISHED BY DOUBLEDAY
a division of Bantam Doubleday Dell Publishing Group, Inc.
666 Fifth Avenue, New York, New York 10103

Anchor Books, Doubleday, and the portrayal of an anchor
are trademarks of Doubleday, a division of Bantam Doubleday
Dell Publishing Group, Inc.

Library of Congress Cataloging-in-Publication Data
Barrett, William, 1913–
Death of the soul.
ISBN 0-385-17327-X (pbk.)
  Includes index.
  1. Soul. 2. Intellect. 3. Civilization, Modern—1950–
BD421.B33   1986   128'.1   82–45317

12 11 10 9 8 7 6 5

For Loretta,
good editor, good friend

Contents

Foreword

Banishing Consciousness

YOU ARE TALKING, let us say, with a close and dear friend. The talk has been animated, and you have both been involved in it, in its varied twists and turns, questions and gropings. But now the conversation begins to stray into more idle channels, and your attention also strays. Not entirely; half your mind can still follow the talk, the other half, in a mood of odd detachment, has fallen into staring at the face and body of your friend as he talks.

Not that there is anything odd or unusual in his appearance; it is the same face, familiar and beloved, as always. It is only that, in looking, your own mind has been invaded with an unusual question. His lips move as he talks, his eyes gleam, and there is the occasional movement of hand and arm as he gestures. All quite as usual. But now the question taking shape in your mind seems to place these ordinary facts in a strange light: Is there really a mind or consciousness behind this physical appearance?

We all have such moments of passing schizophrenia. They come and they go, and normally we do not attach much importance to them. But now this passing mood is buttressed by a solemn body of theory. In our modern world there are philosophers and psychologists who maintain that this human consciousness of ours is an item that can be dispensed with in our theoretical explanations. The theories sometimes differ in their varying degrees of dogmatism or subtlety, but in the end they come to the same thing. We can proceed, they tell us, *as if* the consciousness of the friend does not exist, and we shall find his bodily envelope and its behavior sufficient for all purposes of understanding.

Why this strange fear of human consciousness? Why this uneasiness at admitting it as a clear and evident fact within our human world? Well, for one thing, there is what has been called the "problem of other minds." After all, I do not see the consciousness of my friend, nor do I have any direct sensory datum of it. It is something that I infer; and in this same spirit of hardheaded empiricism I must not treat this consciousness of the other person as a basic datum for explanation. I need not deny its existence outright, but wherever possible, wherever my theoretical ingenuity can manage it, I must proceed "as if" this consciousness were not there.

We may note in passing that this "problem of other minds" is largely a modern invention. The problem is not found among ancient and medieval thinkers. Whatever their other aberrations, these older thinkers did not doubt that we lived in a world that was shared by our own and other minds. But in this modern, scientific age of ours we feel compelled to raise such doubts out of a spirit of what we imagine to be theoretical exactness.

But surely there is something a little strange, even foolish, about this flight from consciousness. Is the consciousness of another person something that we should reasonably expect to *see?* And should we therefore find it questionable and doubtful if we cannot isolate it in any single sense datum? We are plentifully aware of the minds of other people, but in another and more engulfing way: We share them. They are part of the vital flow of life that surrounds and sustains us, in the coming and going of family, friends, and those close to us. We are surrounded by a life larger than ourselves, of which we are an intimate part. Suppose, out of a moment of theoretical austerity, seeking to commit ourselves only to the minimal theory, we strive to consider those close to us "as if" they had no minds and were not conscious, but were only behaving bodies. We would very shortly be schizoid, deranged. Or, to make the illustration as plain and grotesque as possible, you are approaching a moment of tenderness and passion with the woman you love, but for a moment you stop to reflect that theoretically you can treat her words and caresses as if there were no consciousness or mind behind them. That way madness lies!

In short, there is a gap here between theory and life. You entertain and support in argument an intellectual position that you could not possibly live. Such gaps are not uncommon in the Modern Age, but the one we are dealing with is particularly ominous. We have therefore to take a step backward to see how it has come about.

It will soon be the year 2000. The date is awesome, however much we shall probably cover over the occasion with frivolous celebration. After all, it is not every anniversary that we are able to mark as not only the end of a century, but of a millenium. A millennium! That is a long stretch of time, and we are bound to ask ourselves what shape or direction of human history we can mark in those thousand years. Already, in fact, we are near enough to that date that the mind naturally gravitates there as the point from which to look around and take stock of our past.

Of course, there is the nagging question abroad whether this civilization of ours will survive to reach that date. Nowadays, one cannot escape this apocalyptic note. Sometimes we may seem to make too much of it; perhaps we are beginning to develop and indulge a taste for the apocalypse. Sometimes this vision of universal destruction seems to be invoked all too easily as a camouflage for political pleading. No matter; this fear of the apocalypse, whether bogus or genuine, is there, and it is revelatory of our time. It will serve to indicate therefore how we are to situate this century and this millennium historically. After all, it was a very different kind of apocalypse that people waited for in the year 1000.

For the centers of our fear now are technology and science. Because we have developed the technical means to blow our world to bits, we are afraid that in some reckless or berserk moment we might send that world up in flames. In the light, or darkness, of this fear, technology and science emerge as the unique and central facts about our Modern Age.

When did this Modern Age begin? Historical epochs merge into one another, and it may be arbitrary to seek for points of absolute beginning. When, for example, did the Middle Ages begin? When end? It would be futile here to seek an absolute point of division between the past and the epoch that succeeded it. But sometimes there are points at which we can see clearly that by this time something new has already arrived and is bound to transform human history radically. Accordingly, we may take the beginning of our Modern Age to be the early-seventeenth century. For that was the century that created modern science and its accompanying technology; and these two, science and technology, have become, as we have seen, the driving forces within modern civilization.

What is modern science? As often as we have asked and answered this question, we need to rethink it again as we approach the end of the millennium in which that science has decisively transformed human life. We shall have more to say on this question in a later chapter. Suffice it here simply to note that, whatever else it may be, science is an exhibition of the power of the human mind, of its freedom and originality to construct concepts that are not passively found in nature but nevertheless serve to organize our experience of nature. Thus the existence of a body of science is in itself a powerful evidence of human freedom.

Yet here a curious paradox arises. Mechanics was a central part of the new physics; until mechanics was firmly established, physics could not get under way. But the science of mechanics was no sooner founded than a widespread ideology of mechanism followed in its wake. Man is a machine, so the lament goes. The molecules in nature blindly run according to the inalterable mechanical laws of nature; and as our molecules go, so do we. The human mind is a passive and helpless pawn pushed around by the forces of nature. Freedom is an illusion. And this lament was to rise to a crescendo of pessimism during the nineteenth century.

In short, no sooner has science entered the modern world than it becomes dogged by its shadow, scientism. What is this peculiar phenomenon we call scientism? It is not science, any more than the shadow is anywhere identical with the substance of a thing. Nor is science ever evidence of scientism. At most, science merely serves to heat up the imagination of certain minds—and they are not few—who are too prone to sweeping and unqualified generalizations in the first place. Scientism is pseudoscience or misinterpreted science. Its conclusions are sweeping and large, and therefore sometimes pretend to be philosophical. But it is not a part of philosophy, if by philosophy we mean the effort to think soberly within the restrictions that human reflection must impose for itself. No; scientism is neither science nor philosophy, but that peculiarly modern invention and malady—an ideology. And as such, along with other ideologies that beset us, it has become a permanent part of our modern culture.

The science which the seventeenth century sought was chiefly physics, the understanding of physical nature. But at the same time, as the science of nature blossoms, the theories of mind that sprout among philosophers become more paradoxical and at odds with each other. It is as if the thinkers who had reared this dazzling structure of the new science were more and more puzzled to understand the mind that had produced it. The situation has not improved since. In the three and a half centuries since modern science entered the world, we have added immeasurably to our knowledge of physical nature, in scope, depth, and subtlety. But our understanding of human consciousness in this time has become more fragmentary and bizarre, until at present we seem in danger of losing any intelligent grasp of the human mind altogether.

It may be worthwhile, then, to take a step backward and try to see how this situation has come about. For this purpose we need not burden the reader with heavy and excessive historical detail. We shall be pursuing a single theme throughout, and we shall make use of only as much history as may serve to establish its thematic clarity. Nor shall we be seeking here to establish any new "theory of mind," whatever that might be. Such theories, in their ingenuity, sometimes lose their grasp on the very fact of consciousness itself as they seek to replace it by something different; and what we shall be trying here to do is simply to lay hold of the fact itself, the fact of consciousness as a human reality that seems on the way to getting lost in the modern world.

Part I

Gathering of a New Age

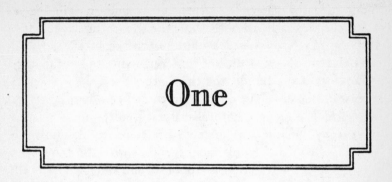

One

A Century of Genius

IT WAS A STRANGE CENTURY, this seventeenth century, which begot our modern epoch. It bristled with energy and genius, but also with contradictions. Yet it was able to contain these contradictions and live with them, and indeed in its own eyes these would not have been taken as contradictions at all. It is only we who see them as such.

For example, it was the century that created modern science, perhaps as great a revolution as ever befell mankind; but the minds of the individuals who created this science were all solidly planted in the mind of God. It is necessary to begin with this salient fact, and indeed one cannot emphasize it too much.

The word "revolution" connotes violence to us: mobs storming in the streets and armies marching against each other. But this was a revolution accomplished silently in the minds of a few men. The great revolutions in thinking, as Nietzsche was later to observe, come silently on dove's feet. And the minds of these revolutionists were in all cases immersed in theology, as the age itself was saturated in theology.

Consider, for example, the three greatest of these scientific geniuses: Kepler, Galileo, and Newton. They hardly viewed the world as a modern naturalist does. Kepler's mind was fascinated by spiritual, or angelic, presences in the universe. Galileo, of course, had his famous run-in with the Inquisition on the subject of the new astronomy, and that has naturally slanted our vision of him. In Bertolt Brecht's play *Galileo*, the great scientist is depicted as a bold freethinker, a dissident spirit, a *libre penseur* in the style of the Enlightenment. Galileo would not have recognized himself in this portrayal. Read his writings and you find that his thought is moving within the mind of God; those laws that he would seek to find within the physical world are, for him, the working of the Divine Mind within nature.

Newton was perhaps the greatest of these great men, the single mind that codified and brought into one unified expression the outlines of the mechanical world that was to dominate the Western mind in the succeeding centuries. Yet when we inquire a little about Newton the man, what do we find? His mind reposed within the prophecies of Daniel, in meditating on which he spent more time than on the problems of mathematical physics. Among the papers he left on his death there were almost a million and a half words on theological and other religious matters. And in his personal life Newton comes across as a man of steady and untroubled faith.

Yet, despite this theological center of their minds, which was in fact in accord with the intensely pious character of the century, these men were doing something very radical that would eventually tear Western civilization loose from its religious moorings. They called the science they were creating "the New Science." What the novelty consisted in they were not yet sure of. (That novelty would be understood in its full depth a century later by the philosopher Kant.) Scientifically, they were very deeply aware of their debt to the ancients—to Greeks like Euclid, Archimedes, and Pappus. The science they were creating would not have been so radical if it had not drawn on that ancient tradition. What T. S. Eliot has said in the context of literature—that the genuinely original creation is that which draws most deeply upon tradition even when it shakes up and transforms this tradition—applies just as surely to science. The whole body of science is a continuous stream from the beginnings of human consciousness, and the genuinely new scientific creation is the one that reaches most deeply into the body of this thought in order to give it some new direction.

Yet, traditionalists as they were, these men were nevertheless also radicals who insisted on calling, and rightly, the science they were creating "the New Science." Wherein did its newness consist? That turns out to be a question that is not easily answered. Indeed, the full philosophical answer was not to be given until the following century, by Immanuel Kant. We shall deal with Kant's answer more fully later, but it is necessary to say a few words here by way of anticipation.

At first glance it might seem that the newness of the New Science lay simply in the fact that it was experimental. Where the ancients had been content to speculate, the moderns insisted on the need of experiment. True as far as it goes; but matters are a little more subtle than this simple reference to experimentation. After all, the scientist does not enter his laboratory with an empty mind and simply start puttering about. The moderns of the seventeenth century did insist on the need of experiments, and best of all, experiments that involved the construction of machines, since precise measurements might be possible in such cases. (From the start, technology and science go together; technology is not merely an incidental application of science, it is there at the root of modern science.)

More than this, in their thought they were constructing nature itself as a machine. The lines of explanation that would be clear and valid for nature itself must be those that they could see clearly in the working of machines they might construct. Mechanics thus became the basic part of physics, and physics the basis of the whole of science. Nature, when we came ultimately to know it, would be construed as a single vast and interlocking machine—the machine of machines.

What was distinctive about mechanics to give it this special place? Mechanics is a science that deals with matter at rest or in motion. But it is not matter in its full, sensuous immediacy that we meet there; rather, it is a matter that has been thoroughly schematized and abstracted—in a word, mathematicized. Thus this New Science that the seventeenth century was proceeding to build was as much mathematical as it was experimental—and thereby hangs a tale, or at least a very serious philosophical lesson. The human mind was in the process of creating, in this New Science, the boldest and most powerful instrument in human history for coping with our material universe. The presence of mind is everywhere in the formation of this science, and yet the results of this science were to be alleged as evidence for some general mechanistic view of the world, according to which the human mind appears as feeble and unfree. That is a paradox and an irony that ever since have haunted the thinking of our modern epoch.

As yet, the founders of the New Science felt no uneasiness about a possible collision between their traditional religious convictions and this mechanistic view of the universe. Indeed, it seemed the simplest and most economical way that God would manage His universe. What more intelligent way to arrange matter and the material universe than as one vast clockwork machine! The uneasiness, when it came, was to appear among the philosophers.

The strictly scientific effort to found mechanics as the basis for physical science passed over into a more general frame of mind—an attitude or disposition that the modern philosopher

Whitehead has aptly labeled "scientific materialism." This was the conviction that the ultimate facts of nature are bits of matter in space, and that all the varied phenomena of experience are to be explained by the movement and configuration of that matter. Moreover, these bits of matter had only the properties that accord with mechanics: mass, extension, solidity, and movement in space. All the other qualities of experience have now a very curious status. The red of the rose or the purple of the sunset are not there where we see them; they come to be somehow (but how?) only in the mind. This whole scheme of thought leaves us ultimately with both a mystery and a paradox, of which Whitehead remarks with fitting irony, "It would seem a curious arrangement of nature that we should see a lot of things that are not there."

Yet, with all its inherent paradoxes, scientific materialism was to become *de facto* the dominant mentality of the West in the three and a half centuries that followed. It ruled not so much as an explicit and articulate philosophy, but more potently as an unspoken attitude, habit, and prejudice of mind. And in this unspoken form, it is still regnant today. The bulk of our research money is still channeled along the paths that accord with this materialism.

For the Christian believer in the seventeenth century who might be tempted into scientific materialism, there was always a special exception for the soul. It was not a natural phenomenon, like other phenomena; it stood outside of nature. But the effect of this adjustment was to leave the soul perched precariously on the edge of matter in strange conjunction with its body. And the precariousness of this perch was to become, as we shall see, more pronounced in the philosophy that followed.

Finally, there was another tension that suddenly emerged in the consciousness of this century. Theologically centered as they were, immersed as their minds were in God, these men of the seventeenth century were in the process of discovering the strangeness of the human presence in this universe. The discoveries of science had begun to show the vastness of the universe beyond the dreams of Greek and medieval civilization.

The theory of Copernicus dislodged once and for all the earth, and humanity with it, from their privileged place at the center of the cosmos. It was not simply that we lost that central place, but that our position in this infinitely extending universe seemed so random and accidental. We were neither at the center, nor the edge, but we had somehow come to be on a small planet nowhere in particular in this teeming universe. That we happened to be here, and not someplace else, seemed just a brute fact, part of the "thrown-ness" of our human existence, as a later philosopher, Heidegger, would call it.

This feeling of cosmic alienation was to be expressed by one of the greatest minds of the great century, Blaise Pascal (1623–62), with a sharpness and poignancy never since equaled:

> When I consider the short duration of my life, swallowed up in the eternity before and after, the little space which I fill, and even can see, engulfed in the infinite immensity of spaces of which I am ignorant and which know me not, I am frightened, and I am astonished at being here rather than there; for there is no reason why here rather than there, why now rather than then. Who has put me here? By whose order and direction have this place and this time been allotted to me? The eternal silence of those infinite spaces frightens me.

Alienation has since become a dominant fact for the modern mind. The word "alienation" itself has come to be thrown about so casually that we have almost trivialized its meaning. In general, we have come to apply the word almost exclusively to forms of social alienation. It is well to remember that the profoundest and most poignant sense of alienation is our cosmic alienation, which is inherent in our human consciousness itself. We are strangers in this universe, and we discover this troubling situation as soon as we begin to be conscious of the world and the universe we inhabit.

Myth, magic, religion, and philosophy seek to deal with this condition in their differing ways. In point of fact, however, philosophers began to take note of this fundamental alienation only in the nineteenth century, when the structures of religious faith had come to be eroded. Whether philosophy by itself—that is, a purely rational effort of mind—can heal this condition, remains to be seen. That is the troubling question that will be at work, sometimes below the surface but sometimes erupting furiously, in the history we shall trace. It is still the great question which this civilization will have to answer for itself.

This brief outline of the seventeenth century does not have quite the shape and emphasis of the picture I absorbed in my early years as a student. My teachers, excellent men, were naturalists and rationalists, confident and at ease in their lack of faith. They saw the opening century of our era along a line of progress that the rationalism of the Enlightenment has imposed on the Western mind. The seventeenth century had created science; if the minds of its creators still reposed within the framework of theology, that was simply a tag of the Middle Ages that still lingered with them, and that would disappear as science progressed, just as other superstitions from the past had disappeared with the advance of knowledge. Sometimes these teachers would speak with a certain irritation at the time Newton had spent on the prophecies of Daniel, as if he might have better spent them on mathematical physics. What further discoveries in physics he might have made, or could have made at the time, they did not say.

It becomes more difficult for us today to accept this view of history along a fixed line of progress. The historical being of man is a more complex and internal matter than any such line would suggest. The being of an epoch realizes human needs and aspirations in a way that is particular to itself. It has to be taken as a whole, in its wholeness, with all of its apparent contradictions fertile and at work. The line of progress is an abstract construction that our historical consciousness has projected, but the historical being of mankind is a deeper fact of our being than any abstraction we construct. The seventeenth century was what it was; it cannot be taken simply as a way station between the Middle Ages and our Modern (scientific) Age. History is, fundamentally, the adventure of human consciousness. Our modern adventure began with the seventeenth century, but that earlier age has not vanished like a marker on a line that we have passed; it is still present, with all its paradoxes and tensions, in the uncertainties and malaise of our modern consciousness. Our civilization may in the future—who knows?—move to the point where it will regret that the minds of its scientists are not, like Newton's, involved with the prophecies of Daniel or some other religious matter.

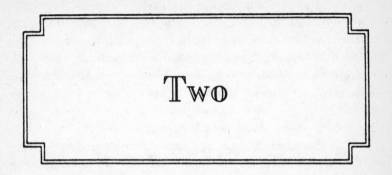

Two

Soul and Reason

THE RIFT between ourselves and the cosmos—between subject and object—is, then, one troubling legacy that the seventeenth century bequeathed to us. Contemporary philosophers, of all schools, and in their differing ways, have protested against this subject-object split. They would like, if possible, to get rid of these troubling notions altogether. And so the philosophers at the beginning of our epoch, particularly Descartes, are taxed with having introduced an unnecessary dichotomy into our thinking.

But before we conclude that they had simply concocted a distinction that was unnecessary, we had better take a more objective look at the facts that impelled Descartes and the others along their path. The sense that there is somehow an uneasy tension between our human consciousness and the universe was not a subjective whim on the part of these thinkers. In fact, it is objectivity as such that forces us back on our own subjectivity as we confront the universe. The scientists of the seventeenth century had just begun to sift the astronomical evidence of our dwindling place in the cosmos. But, for us, the universe, in its detail, has expanded quite beyond what even their imaginations could envision. It is we, on the contrary, whose imaginations have become more callous. I pick up, for example, a little book of star maps that is an old companion of mine on my night walks, and I learn:

We, on this earth of ours, are embedded in the great system of stars which is called our galaxy. Shaped somewhat like a pocket watch, the galaxy is about a hundred thousand light-years in diameter, perhaps fifteen thousand light-years thick, and contains approximately a hundred billion stars.

The seventeenth century was not yet familiar with the notion of a light-year, but we throw around light-years (a light-year, by the way, happens to be approximately six trillion miles!) with the casualness of our national debt.

Copernicus dislodged the earth from the center and showed it revolving about the sun. But this sun of ours, a small star, itself revolves with other stars within its galaxy, completing a revolution about once every two hundred fifty million years. But the vistas of distance only begin here. We can think of our galaxy (with its hundred billion stars) as our "island" in the ocean of emptiness which is the whole universe. There are millions of other "islands" known, and undoubtedly countless millions of others not yet seen. Each galaxy consists of billions of stars and each is some one or two million light-years from its nearest neighbors.

And so on, and so forth, vista upon vista and motion upon interlocking motion—until the mind reels before this picture it cannot assemble.

Meanwhile, I sit late at night, my old dog snoring at my feet, and another series of images flashes before my mind. On this tiny planet of ours, lost in space, life somehow arose and passed through the various stages of evolution to arrive at our human species. And there flicker before my mind images of the long and tormented history of humankind, from its primitive beginnings, the rise and fall of empires and dynasties, until the present global civilization that now teeters on the edge of the abyss. What does all that troubled history *mean* against this cosmic background? And my own tiny consciousness, which is all I have lighting up briefly here in the night— what does it mean when set against that history and that cosmos? And so I am forced back into the anguish that Pascal felt over three hundred years ago.

Meanwhile my dog continues to sleep peacefully at my feet. She is not troubled by such questions; there is no rift, division, or dualism within her being, bound as it is within the cycle of instinct. That rift emerges within our human consciousness as soon as we are exposed to those questions. And man is the dualistic animal in the sense that he cannot escape these questions that wrench him out of the complacent security of his instinctual existence.

It is necessary to make at least this preliminary defense of dualism, at least as a native tendency of our human being, before we pass on to see what kind of doctrine philosophers make of it.

But there is more to this moment than a brief flare-up of a consciousness—any consciousness—confronting its world. The "I" that cogitates here (while my dog goes on sleeping) drags a history and memories with it. It is a concrete self, dense, particular, unique—myself, in short—and I cannot escape it. I have lived within it, through it, and seemingly beyond it, but if so only by means of it. My feelings and emotions go on inseparable from my thoughts, coloring them, and I am aware of this body, *my* body, whose presence has always been here, penetrating thought. For aeons of time, the universe existed without me, and will continue to exist for aeons after I am gone; and measured now against time, rather than space, I am even more poignantly aware of the brief finitude of my being. And yet this "I" that will someday vanish must have for me a reality incomparable with any other. The thought of its finitude provokes me now to an uneasy sense of all my sins and shortcomings, misdeeds and omissions, failings and faintheartedness. And I am moved, once again and even more intensely, to ask, What meaning can this faltering moral existence of mine have? Not the "meaning of life" as a universal formula, but *my* particular meaning. In short, this *I* that emerges, but remains also hidden, is a concrete self, inescapably moral and emotional as well as cogitative; and not in the sense that morality and feeling are somehow pasted on or added to my thinking; they are there at the roots of the I.

Let us turn now to the philosophers to see how much of this concrete density of the self gets into their thought. We shall find in some cases, I am afraid, that only a thin trickle of that self is allowed to pass through the filters of their reflection.

DESCARTES: THE SOLITARY MIND

It is fitting that we begin this brief sketch of a history with the figure of Descartes (1596–1650). He is the thinker who projects human consciousness to the center of philosophy. And our central theme here, lest the reader forget, is the drama of mind within our modern Western civilization.

The consciousness that Descartes projects is a solitary one: the self-consciousness of the philosopher meditating alone in his room. Yet he was anything but a cloistered figure. He was very much a man of his time; and in his thinking, as well as his life, he illustrates both the remarkable unity and the remarkable variety of the mind of the seventeenth century.

The intellectual unity of that period is very real despite the intellectual and personal differences of the individuals involved. There is, first, the overriding passion for mathematical physics, which Descartes shared along with his other intellectual contemporaries. His fundamental contribution to science was the invention of analytic geometry, without which the later development of the calculus, the supreme mathematical tool in the exploration of nature, by Newton and Leibnitz, would not have been possible. And if in his other adventures in science, he did not equal the accomplishments of such figures as Galileo and Newton, he continued as an active proselytizer of the New Science.

But Descartes is more than a mind engrossed in questions of science and philosophy. He is also something of a man of action. In this respect, he is very much a man of the Renaissance, with something of the flash and dare of that period about him, even though by temperament he had more than a touch of shrewdness and coolness. It was a turbulent time, and Descartes in his own fashion shared in it. From 1618 to 1628, from his twenty-second to his thirty-second years, he served as a volunteer in the armies of Europe: first with the army of the prince of Orange in the Netherlands and then in the Bavarian Army. It was a time when the cannon was emerging as a potent weapon of war; and Descartes, as a mathematician, could interest himself in some of the mathematical problems of projectiles.

But at this time the supreme adventure of his life is yet to come, and it will come in the life of thought, not action. In 1629 he retires to an inn in Holland and goes into seclusion. He will put together the meditations that have been with him off and on during his whole life: he will build what will come to be known as the Cartesian system. It is thus in exploring his own solitude that he becomes the supreme adventurer. And this quality of bold adventure about his thinking, the sense of launching himself into a new path, is still there for us; it comes alive and captures us whenever we pick up his text, however much we have been exposed to the carpings of some modern critics against "Cartesianism" and its errors.

What is this new beginning that he proposes for philosophy? Descartes will start with the primary fact of his own consciousness—the I, the ego, which thinks, and lights up his solitude in the inn in Holland where he has come to find refuge from the wars of his time.

It is necessary to pause for a moment over this solitary and daring step. We have to remind ourselves of the intellectual background of the time from which Descartes speaks. We think of the seventeenth century as a period of intellectual advance, which it certainly was, but in so doing we sometimes forget the uncertainty and doubt that these bold new theories introduced into the ordinary ways of seeing the world. The ordinary world of the senses does not seem any longer to be the true world. Consider the Copernican theory, that the earth goes around the sun, as a simple example in point. We see the sun rise in the east, circle the heavens, and set in the west. But now this ordinary view of the senses is to be cast into uncertainty by the new theory.

Descartes would meet these uncertainties head-on. Even if these ordinary objects in his room in the inn do not really exist as they appear to, or even do not exist at all, there is no doubt of the consciousness that perceives them. That consciousness has to be there in order to be deceived. For the philosopher, then, the fact of consciousness must be granted priority over the objects of the external world. Indeed, the conscious subject, the conscious "I," must be taken as the starting point for philosophy.

This bold step of Descartes was to meet with varied responses from philosophers in the modern period. We shall be dealing with that reception more in detail later, but a brief preliminary indication here may underline the significance of the issue. At the beginning of the nineteenth century, only a little more than a century and a half ago, the German philosopher Hegel, an idealist, could celebrate this turn Descartes had taken as decisive for human thinking. Hitherto, Hegel writes, philosophy has been like a ship sailing over the oceans, but now, with Descartes, the ship has come at last into harbor and discovered its native soil and subject matter: the conscious subject, the I and its subjectivity. But a century after

Hegel, in our own time, the tables have been turned, and you would be hard put to find any glowing tribute to Descartes on this particular point. Idealism, as a systematic philosophy, has virtually ceased to be; the two prevailing philosophies of our time are phenomenology and analytic philosophy, and both decry the errors of what they call "Cartesianism." If you go from philosophers as different as the phenomenologist Martin Heidegger to the analyst Gilbert Ryle, however they may differ on other points, they seem at least united (though it may be for quite different reasons) in their condemnation of the specter of Cartesianism. What is the significance of this historic shift? I suggest that it may be one more indication of how far our civilization has moved away from concern with the personal subject toward an impersonal objectivity.

But does Descartes really bring the actual and concrete subject into philosophy? The I that lives and breathes in intimacy with its body, enmeshed in memories, anxious about death, and possibly hoping, if it dare, for some kind of salvation? No; he is a philosopher pursuing a particular theme, the search for certainty, and the poor ego is only a thematic instrument, though an indispensable one, in the search. Thus Descartes launches himself on his famous systematic doubt, through the course of which the ego remains as an unshakable point of departure and return. I may doubt the existence of objects in the external world, but I cannot doubt my own consciousness of them. If I doubt the existence of my own consciousness, the doubt itself is a conscious act. So the ego comes back upon itself in its own unshakable self-certainty, shining luminously against a dubitable world.

But having thus extracted the mind from its world, Descartes is hard put to get it back into the world. For that purpose he must invoke the help of God. The laborious doubt has left him with a painful sense of his own finitude and imperfections, but he has also the idea of a Perfect Being, complete and self-grounding, embracing all reality. This idea cannot come from himself, imperfect as he is, and therefore must have been produced in him by this Perfect Being itself. Moreover, being perfect, God must exist, since nonexistence would be an imperfection.

Such is Descartes's version of the ontological argument for the existence of God, which has run its varied course through the history of philosophy ever since St. Anselm introduced it, though in a different formulation, back in the twelfth century. In fact, it is not really an argument at all, and its varied formulations in pseudo-demonstrative form often mask what it really is. Rather than an argument, it is an intuition, valid and compelling for some minds as soon as they begin to reflect upon the mystery of existence. This is the intuition that finite existence cannot just float but must be grounded in some all-encompassing and self-grounding Being. Cardinal Newman, a great religious writer though not a philosopher, states it as the beginning article of his faith in his *Apologia:*

> Starting then with the being of a God, which, as I have said, is as certain to me as the certainty of my own existence . . .

This is the direct expression of religious feeling, without the web of philosophical argumentation Descartes spins about it. Yet it would be a mistake to think that Descartes's reasoning, for him in his time and place, does not carry a similar religious content.

Armed, then, with the premise that there is a God, Descartes can now set about restoring the ego to the world from which his systematic doubt had torn it. Since God is good, he would not have created our minds so that they are deceived about the world around them. If we use our faculties properly, we can have valid knowledge of the external world. And thus Descartes has solved his epistemological problem.

But notice that this ego that is to be restored to its world is only an abstract ego, the *ego cogitans,* or thinking ego, the ego as knower or scientist, and not the concrete self that you and I are. How is this concrete self, with all its physical, sensuous, and emotional life, to be restored to the Cartesian world? And

here the problems of Descartes's dualism—the dualism between body and mind—become particularly acute.

The soul is more inclusive, more encompassing, than reason.
We have a new and more powerful reason to be aware of this
with the emergence of psychoanalysis in our century.
"Psyche" in Greek means soul—a meaning we should not let
ourselves forget—and psychoanalysis, accordingly, is a therapy that deals with the individual soul. I am not drawing here
on any of the specific theories of psychoanalysis, which are in
any case still in a state of exploration and flux; I wish simply
to call attention, instead, to the historical fact that psychoanalysis did arrive on the scene and has become, at least in
some quarters, a recognized form of therapy. We have to ask
ourselves what that arrival signifies.

Psychoanalysts are trained in medical faculties, but they do
not treat physical illness. They deal with troubled patients,
but the trouble is not physical or bodily, it is a trouble of the
psyche, though it may have physical consequences. And usually it is not rational; or if reason does enter into the process,
it has, more often than not, become twisted or blinded by
emotional undercurrents. For the patient, emotional distress
may be as real as a physical toothache, and all the more dis-
tressing since it cannot be so easily located. And usually his
reason is quite powerless against it.

Descartes's picture of the human mind looks curiously inadequate here. The *ego cogitans,* the rational and thinking ego,
which Descartes had made the very center and essence of the
human soul, has in the psychoanalytic process discovered that
it is contained and invaded by forces unknown to itself. The
psyche, or soul, turns out to be very much more than reason.
And with the historical appearance of psychoanalysis it is as if
the psyche, long submerged by our culture, has become very
real and has resurfaced.

Oddly enough, the trouble with the Cartesian dualism
comes from the side of the body. The body, as Descartes con-
ceives it, is not such that it can accommodate the soul. It

cannot, so to speak, be penetrated by the soul; it can only remain in external contact with it. This body is not the physical body, our physical body, as we know it in our daily intimacy with it. It is the body of physics—that is, of the science of physics; a piece of matter, and particularly as Descartes conceived of matter. But the body of physics is remote and unknown to us and is not the body we live in in our day-to-day existence. The body we know is rarely sharply distinguishable from the soul: in our moods and feelings we are not often sure what part is physical and what not. There is no sharp dividing line between. The life of flesh and blood is particularly focused about the feelings and emotions. So long as there is no adequate conception of the concrete or lived body, our theories of mind cannot deal adequately with the life of feeling.

To be sure, Descartes went ahead and wrote a *Treatise on the Passions*. That was part of the adventurer and conquistador in him. Having established the foundation of the *ego cogitans*, the thinking ego, he must now let that ego look around, with an imperialistic eye, to claim the adjacent territory. His treatise is, consequently, a strange and yet revealing work. The feelings and emotions are seen from the privileged position of reasoning. Thus they are seen from the outside, objectively, as objects that are to be noted, but not as states of being that we subjectively live. The feelings are alien and other, rather like pets in this house that the master, Reason, must keep in order. The I that feels and suffers is an object to be looked at. So a particular model of mind became embedded in Western culture at the very beginning of the Modern Age and has really persisted with us since.

The soul in Descartes is still a Christian soul; though the lineaments may sometimes be faint, they are still there. But it is a Christian soul that has undergone another crucifixion: this time on the cross of mathematical physics.

A UNIVERSE OF SOULS: LEIBNITZ

It is appropriate that the next step in our brief saga of mind in Western civilization take us to the figure of Leibnitz. He radically revises and completes the thinking of Descartes on the human soul; and, I suggest, might revise some of our contemporary thinking on this subject if we but have the intellectual imagination to follow his bold speculations.

Leibnitz comes on the scene two generations after Descartes, and much has happened in those intervening years. For one thing, the outlines and structure of the New Science have become established, and one can now see the shape of the world that this new vision constructs. Leibnitz is to call attention to the philosophical shadows that lurk about the Newtonian picture of the world. He thus raises some basic questions that we have had to wrestle with once again in our present century.

Gottfried Wilhelm Leibnitz (1646–1716) would have been an extraordinary figure at any time. In a "century of genius" he stands out as perhaps its most many-sided mind. There seems almost no field of learning that he did not touch and adorn: science, mathematics, philosophy, theology, jurisprudence, and history. And more than this immersion in various fields of learning, he maintained contact with the best minds of his time. He visited the Royal Society in England, and he was a diligent and prolific correspondent. He thus brings before us in a striking way the fact that the Western mind in the seventeenth century, despite the divergence of individual views, had a kind of unity of outlook and background that we have never quite known again.

But there is one particular field of his learning that his commentators sometimes forget and to which we must now call attention: the field of philosophy itself. Leibnitz was, to put it bluntly, the best-educated philosopher of his period—

and by this I mean educated within philosophy itself. Descartes's philosophical background was what he had picked up from the Jesuits at La Flèche; Leibnitz read omnivorously on his own in the history of philosophy and digested thoroughly what he read. While many of his contemporaries were engaged in prying themselves aggressively loose from the Middle Ages, Leibnitz read the medieval Scholastics sympathetically and through them was able to reach back to a direct understanding of Aristotle (which the seventeenth century had lost) and of the Greeks; and he could appreciate that the ancient views of nature might have a validity that the New Science was overlooking. Generally, indeed, he saw the continuity of medieval with Greek philosophy and thus had a sense of the unity of Western thought that was lacking in most of his contemporaries.

At the same time, he was thoroughly conversant with the New Science, in which he was himself a powerful innovator. He was cocreator, with Newton, of the calculus, the most powerful mathematical tool of the Modern Age. On the other hand, he was a diligent student of Christian theology, which he took seriously as theory and wove into the body of his philosophy. Only a mind of great speculative power and daring could fuse such diverse elements; Leibnitz was such a mind. He was in some ways the speculative metaphysician par excellence, the resources and depth of whose thought we have only begun to sift. Also, he was perhaps the last of the great Christian philosophers, in the sense that the fullness of the Christian life is present to his thought, whereas less than a century later, in Kant, this Christian presence has already become diluted. The life of grace, for example, is taken by Leibnitz as a fact, and unless we appreciate this we do not comprehend his philosophy.

What is wrong with Descartes's conception of the body? A body is a chunk of matter. But what is matter? The essence of matter, according to Descartes, is simply extension—it fills space. Here Leibnitz bridles. The nature of extension is simply that a part, any part, is external to any other. How do they cohere as one body? The desk across the room, for example, a piece of brown wood, extends from one bounding surface to another. But simply as extension, any part you choose is external to any other, and so the table would fall apart into a disconnected heap of many parts. But it is in fact *one* body, one table, and there must be some unifying energy that makes it one. And here we pass from the inert notion of matter to the notion of energy.

The universe constructed by the New Science and codified by Newton is essentially an inertial universe; against this, Leibnitz would present us an energic universe. The notion of energy is one of the most difficult to grasp conceptually, for our minds find it easier to think of objects and bodies. Even in modern physics, where the notion of energy becomes basic to matter, today there is only a remote conception of energy, surrounded by certain *ad hoc* conditions to secure quantitative calculation and, above all, a constant quantity of energy in the universe. But energy as we know it directly, in the flow of psychic energy in ourselves, does not seem subject to such constancy. It waxes or wanes as this or that idea or event in our life charges us with energy or makes us droop in despondency.

Let us try to follow Leibnitz here in the speculative hints he furnishes. If the characteristic of the inertial or mechanical universe is that motion is never originated but only continued, then, in the energic universe, on the other hand, there are genuine beginnings. Energy can be self-generating. That is a hard notion for us to get used to, but let us grope for a while with it. After all, the two theories of mind that divide philosophers at the beginning of our Modern Age—that the mind is active (Continental philosophers) or that it is essentially passive (British philosophers)—are involved here. For if it be claimed that the mind is active, appropriating experience or directing its response thereto, we may well ask whence it generates the energy of that activity.

It is in the light (or darkness) of this notion of energy, I suggest, that we must approach Leibnitz's monadology. We might try the following tack: Let us imagine a universe that would be the antithesis of the materialist picture of the world. The ultimate items of the world, for the materialist, are atoms moving in the void of space. As these atoms bounce off one another, they transmit motion; but otherwise motion is never originated. Now suppose we turn this materialist scheme inside out. Instead of matter, we posit spirit as the ultimate stuff of the world, and instead of *atoms* we now have Leibnitzian *monads*. These monads are centers of energy in an energic universe. We have, then, a universe of souls, though souls at differing levels of spirit and energy. The human self, for example, as an individual soul, is a monad, but it is also a community of monads, as it embraces within itself the various units and substructures that make up our human being.

Monads in place of atoms! This is not an idle substitution. How different these monads are from the atoms of materialism, those solid and tiny billiard balls that are essentially inert and passive and move only as they suffer an impact from outside! The monads, on the other hand, generate their own destiny. As such, I propose now, the monad may be taken as a speculative model of the human soul or self. A speculative model, of course, is not an empirical concept. But, in its own way, it may be just as important, for it may give us the lead in what direction to look in order to fabricate our empirical concepts and theories.

The self as a Leibnitzian monad! It may not be such a fantastic idea as you might first think if you begin now to look around at the people, the human souls, you know. A wife of forty years unexpectedly dies, and you are left with memories and old photographs. Some of those photographs are from a time before you knew her, from childhood and early girlhood. No matter. You see the same soul carving her unique destiny

through time. Or you watch children, your own and others'.
They are different from the cradle; and growing up in the
same household and under similar conditions, they pursue
vastly different paths through life. Environmentalists, who
wish to view us as merely the product shaped by our conditioning, are willing sometimes to concede grudgingly that individuals may select different stimuli in their environment to
respond to. But if the psyche, or soul, selects, then it is *active*
and not merely passive, and insofar as it generates its own
destiny. And further than this, it may be active not merely in
selecting among its varied stimuli; it may go out of its way to
seek out and generate the stimuli, to which it then responds. I
have a friend who is a philosopher—a genuine one, who lives
his subject. Nothing in his background led him this way; all
his early circumstances should have led him in another direction; as a boy, he had not the least idea of what philosophy
was and what it was he might be seeking. The psyche had to
go out of its way (out of its environment) to find out what it
was it sought. Self-originating activity!

What I am proposing, in short, is another concept of the
self than the model of stimulus response that has now become
locked into our psychological science. The notions of stimulus
and response do indeed have their power and usefulness in
considerable areas of our human experience, but to take them
as the final word on our human condition is shortsighted. And
when we toss around, as we often do now, the terms stimulus
and response too easily and mechanically, we are in fact de-
scending into one of the forms of psychobabble which has
become such a menace in our culture.

For a moment, all this might look like Jean-Paul Sartre's
view of the self as a project freely created by each of us. In
fact, it is at the farthest remove from it. For one thing, Sartre
denies the existence of the unconscious, while Leibnitz (and
let this be remembered to his credit) is one of the first and few
philosophers who acknowledges the reality of the unconscious
mind. Our freedom as a spiritual being is what issues from the

deeper regions of ourselves, and our squabbling consciousness may have to learn to attune itself with that depth and extract wisdom from it. Sartre's is one more modern instance of a view of mind that has cut itself off from the concrete self. (And in this he is one with certain modern analytic philosophers, though he comes at the matter from a very different angle from theirs.) Consequently, his view of freedom as absolute and arbitrary—the free project by which we create a self, any self we fancy—really floats in the void. Authentic freedom lies in a dialectical transaction, give and take, between conscious and unconscious, between necessary and arbitrary choice.

How, then, are we to try to conceive of this concrete monad, the self that each of us is? First of all, it is a psychophysical unit. What we call body and what we call soul are abstractions, aspects of one unitary reality and process. In our ordinary experience (which must always be our primary point of departure and return) we cannot always tell where body ends and soul begins. In most of our moods, we cannot disentangle where the physical ends and the mental begins. They interpenetrate. Likewise, the center of this monad we have to conceive as lying below the level of consciousness. It is a center of energy that issues in psychic or physical energy, and, again, neither of these two are experienced separately. As our mood lifts, the body soars with it, and as our body sags, the spirit droops with it.

Naturally, in this view the body is no longer an alien chunk of matter, à la Descartes, on which the soul precariously perches. The body here is spiritualized; and perhaps it is with this spiritualization of the body that our eventual honoring of the soul will have to begin. For one thing, the body labors mightily in behalf of the soul—to make anything like a spiritual life possible. In his charming and profound book *The Lives of a Cell*, Dr. Lewis Thomas points out that the notion of man cutting himself off from nature is a myth. Amid our man-made cages of steel and glass we still live within the teeming welter of microbic life. As a layperson, I am always over-

whelmed with awe and terror when I see moving pictures of
submicroscopic life—of cells and bacilli attacking and devour-
ing each other with such stark violence. I wonder how it is
that we ourselves, as rather large-size animals, can survive in
such a jungle of microbic life. Only the marvelous organiza-
tion of our human body permits us to survive. That organiza-
tion is a society of cells in turn colonized by microbic life that
may have its independent genetic structure and descent but
nevertheless works to our advantage. The mitochondria, for
example, colonize us, and thus could be regarded as parasites,
but they perform an indispensable service in the process of
oxidation within the cell. Surely it was one of the most extraordinary steps in the process of evolution to have produced
something like the human body as a delicately organized society, a balanced adjustment, within the welter of submicroscopic life, both being used by and using that life—a diplo-
matic arrangement, as it were, of the balance of power. It was
one of nature's grandest steps in the direction of spirit. It is
what makes the spiritual life, so far as we can know it, at all
possible.

Nature and spirit thus meet in the psychophysical unit that
each of us is. The monads are spiritual entities.

"WHY IS THERE ANYTHING AT ALL, RATHER THAN NOTHING?"

As one side of Leibnitz's extraordinary mind is the richness
of metaphysical imagination that could envisage a universe of
organisms within organisms, so the other side is a unique capacity for simplicity and logical incisiveness. And nowhere is
this capacity for going simply and directly to the heart of an
issue exhibited more clearly than in his handling of the arguments for the existence of God, especially when we compare
him here with the tradition of philosophers before him.

Consider, for example, the question with which this section

opens. It is the question that lurks behind all traditional arguments for God, and yet it comes out clearly into the open only
with Leibnitz. The tradition begins with Aristotle, and in one
sense we have always to return to him when we take up the
matter. In Aristotle, moreover, we feel there is no *parti pris*,
no special "religious yearning" clamoring to be justified by his
arguments. They are the result of the free play of the human
mind: as soon as that mind begins to reflect on the world
around it, it seeks for causes or reasons, and it is led inevitably
in the direction of seeking an ultimate cause or ground. We
have to keep this free and detached intellectual aspect of the
question throughout. But our mental life is not so easily com-
partmentalized, as we have already begun to see in the case of
the ego and Descartes; and the question of God, as we shall
see later, when we come to Kant, cannot be isolated from
other portions of our being.

Moreover, Aristotle's arguments for God, as the Prime
Mover, seem to us too much tied to his own cosmology—to
the tidy finite universe of concentric spheres that Greek astronomy had consigned to his philosophic use. The seventeenth century broke through that tidy universe, and its imagination envisioned a much vaster and possibly infinite
universe. Leibnitz speaks from the center of this new consciousness. He cuts through any assumptions about a finite
universe with a Prime Mover who is first in the series. Hence
his arguments have at once a greater generality and a more
radical simplicity.

"Why is there anything at all, rather than nothing?" This,
then, is our root question. It is the question of questions, says
Heidegger the existentialist, who nevertheless lets it lurk
broodingly in the background but never comes to grips with
it. The question permeates more of our ordinary life than the
average person is aware of. It is there in our ordinary moods
even when it is not intellectually articulated. In a moment of
personal confusion and discontent, for example, we may catch
a flash of our whole life and murmur, "Why was I ever born?"

And in that movement our uneasiness may invest our whole world: why this world, or for that matter, any world at all? Our moods are often more total and metaphysical than we like to think.

But *why* is also the word that demands an explanation. *Why* means we are seeking for a cause or reason. The things in the world that we encounter are brought into existence by other things or conditions. They are contingent beings. A contingent being is one whose existence is derived from beings other than itself. All the things in nature that we know of are contingent. Animals are begotten, born, and die; sun and moon and stars come into being through natural causes and may perish; the so-called "everlasting hills" are brought into existence by geological convulsions and after aeons of time can be eroded away. Leibnitz begins his argument, then, with this simple and familiar idea of contingent being, to which he adds an axiom, the *principle of sufficient reason*. This principle states that there is no fact without a sufficient reason why it exists and is so rather than otherwise. The principle, as such, is not really arcane or obscure; it states the ordinary procedures of our mind when we encounter any particular fact in the world. We ask for a cause or explanation; we would not be satisfied if told flatly that there is no cause or reason, it just happens to be the case.

Let us begin, then, with any particular contingent being, A. As contingent, A will have a cause external to itself, B. B, in turn, is produced by C. Etc., etc. Does the chain go on endlessly, or does it have a first link, a first cause? Let us not make things easier for ourselves; let us suppose that there is no first link, that the chain is infinite.

But this infinite chain itself—what of it? Each link in the chain is contingent, and thus the whole chain is itself a contingent fact. And as contingent, it must have some cause external to itself. Where do we look for it? Suppose there is another chain that has produced our first chain. So scientists speak of one universe begetting another, or one cosmic epoch producing its successor. But this latter chain? It, too, will require a cause. And so we could go from chain to chain to chain, and so on and so forth . . .

Let us then imagine an infinite number of infinite chains. Where do we now stand? We are left with our original mystery. Why does anything at all exist? Why do all those chains, infinite upon infinite, exist at all? So long as we remain within the realm of contingent being, we go from link to link and chain to chain but never find an answer to the mystery of existence. Scientific explanation can only go from particular link to particular link; it can never deal with the whole.

We are faced, then, with two alternatives from which we may choose:

1. We can say there is no reason. But if we choose this alternative, we cannot do so in the style of the cavalier or superficial atheist who does not pause for a moment at the enormity he is accepting. For it is an enormity: we do not say elsewhere, of any particular fact, that there is no explanatory cause or reason, the fact just simply happens to be there; but in this case, confronted by the most enormous fact of all, the universe, we would be willing to say it just happens to be there. We need to have the intellectual imagination of Nietzsche to grasp how audacious and staggering is the hypothesis of atheism. For if we say the world is without a reason, then it becomes absurd, and the whole of existence, and we along with it, absurd. We have then to accept the absurdity of life, as some of the existentialists have spoken of it, and learn to live with that absurdity.

Still, there is no logical impossibility in this alternative; and we can accept it without logical contradiction, however our habits and extincts may rebel against it.

OR 2. We can affirm that there is a reason or cause why all those chains upon chains of beings exist. But if we make this choice, we have to step outside of the realm of contingent beings. So long as we remain within the sequence of contingent beings, there is no sufficient reason why the whole exists. We have to posit a being of another order, a *necessary being*, the ground of whose existence lies not in another or others but in itself. And this necessary being will be what, on the level of faith and worship, the religious consciousness has called God.

Here, too, however, as in the case of the atheist, the believer has to recognize the intellectual audacity of the step he has taken. What is this necessary being? Do we have any adequate idea of it? We answer a mystery by positing a mystery. We can, of course, define a necessary being negatively by simply saying that it is a noncontingent being. But does this purely verbal definition give us any constructive concept of the thing we are talking about?

These are the questions that Immanuel Kant was to bring forward a little less than a century later. The confrontation of Leibnitz and Kant on the arguments for God is one of the decisive moments in intellectual history, and probably shaped the modern mind more than all the noise of wars and revolutions. We postpone our discussion of it to a later chapter.

Meanwhile, to bring this rather devious chapter to a summation, we notice that the question of the soul is persistently connected with two other items:

1. the soul and its body;
2. the soul and God.

The significance of the first, we may find, surprisingly enough and from the most unsuspected quarters, is that the modern mind (Leibnitz excepted) tends to build a notion of disembodied mind. As for the second, the question arises whether the soul, as such, can ever be truly human unless it is seeking God. And on that turns the further question, which Nietzsche was to claim as central to our history, whether mankind can survive as godless. That still remains to be seen.

Three

The Puzzles of Sensation

WHAT FORMS A NATIONAL CHARACTER, what makes one people different from another, may be difficult and perhaps impossible to determine; but the fact of such national differences is undeniably and plainly there. And these differences are plainly there by the seventeenth century and the beginning of our Modern Age. By that time the British already considered themselves different from the peoples of the Continent. Thus the English Channel divides not merely two bodies of land but two types of mind. And this difference in character is clearly exhibited in the kind of philosophy that will be pursued in the British Isles.

The British profess a certain distrust of intellectuals and the intellect. They are a practical people, and they prefer forthright common sense to the intricacies of the French or Germans. Whether or not this gift for practicality and plain sense was the faculty responsible, it is clearly at work in the greatest creation of the British genius: liberal democratic government. And the triumph of this character is not merely that it conceived free government as an idea, but that it embodied it and set it to work in stable form. It took the turmoil of a century, including civil war, to bring it about, but by the end of the seventeenth century, England had firmly laid down the structure of a free society, which continued to develop during the following two centuries. We no longer take this achievement of political democracy quite for granted, as we once might have done. As the totalitarian forces encircle us, we can imagine that in their ultimate victory the period of liberty—British liberty, if you will—might be only a momentary and vanished light against the long darkness. Even so, in the long history of humanity it would have been Britain's "finest hour," to use Winston Churchill's phrase for the embattled British in the years of the Second World War.

THE TWO WORLDS

John Locke (1632–1704) was the philosopher of the British political revolution, and perhaps he remains still the foremost spokesman for classical liberalism. But our theme points elsewhere, and we do not follow him through the high road of political philosophy, but in his more devious journey through the intricacies of the human soul. He will exhibit the same British traits there: the sense of fact, plain speech, and common sense. Thus his procedure, he tells us, is "the plain historical method": he will understand the operations of the mind by tracing the genesis of its ideas from sensations. All our ideas come from sensations and are tested again by the simple appeal to sensation. This is the core of empiricism as a philosophic position, and Locke's is the first step toward a systematic formulation of empiricist doctrine. But, from the start, there are certain snags to this formulation.

For one thing, sensation provides us with the materials of thought, but the mind seems to do something with these materials, combining and recombining them. Is the mind active or not; does it do something on its own or is it merely passive before the flood of sensations? This is a cardinal question, and on it turns the question of human freedom. For if the mind is active to form judgments of its own, it is possible that it may also initiate actions consequent upon those judgments. Locke's language is ambiguous here, but he tends toward the passivity of mind. That, indeed, is the empiricist tendency generally. Later on, a more hard-nosed empiricism would advance a theory of the association of ideas, according to which the sensations combine and de-combine according to a mechanism of their own, so that we have here a thorough mechanical and deterministic model of the mind. Locke does not go that far, but his emphasis suggests it.

But what is this "mind" that we are talking of? All ideas, says the empiricist, originate in sensations. What, then, are the sensations that correspond to our idea of mind? Does the mind ever exhibit itself in sensation at all? Or is it a nonsensuous entity grasped directly by some intuition other than sensation?

Locke, of course, is a believing Christian, and he carries with him the traditional view of the soul as an immaterial and immortal substance. That is a constraining framework outside of which his empiricism must work. His world is bifurcated, or split in two. There is the region where empiricism holds sway and every idea is to be traced to its genesis in sensation, and the region where the traditional doctrine about the soul dwells dimly. They touch only in that the second is a barrier, at least as far as philosophical analysis is concerned, to the first. His empiricism is thus incomplete and halfhearted.

There is also another, and graver, split in Locke's world of experience, and it comes from the opposite direction from traditional religion: the New Science. By the time of Locke, modern physics was securely on the scene. The science of mechanics had just been codified by Newton, and it presented a complete mechanical system of the world. This was a world in which the qualities of mass, length (extension), and motion were basic. Accordingly they became basic to Locke, and he introduced his famous distinction between primary and secondary qualities. The primary qualities—solidity, extension, shape, mobility—really belong to bodies, and so are objectively real. The secondary are the qualities of color, sound, taste, and the rest; they do not really belong to the world of bodies outside us; they are only subjective effects produced in our minds by the primary qualities in bodies. The shape and mass of the red rose are in the rose itself, but the red of the rose is only in our minds, a mere subjective effect. The world of experience is thus arbitrarily split by a distinction between reality—what is really real—and appearance. The bifurcation is arbitrary, because if we follow experience itself (which the empiricist is professing to do), we are not led to make that distinction: the red of the rose, the green of the leaves, the orange of the sunset are so plainly there in our world and not in our mind. The bifurcation is the result of an a priori assumption on Locke's part: the assumption that the world of physics, the world of material science, gives us the real and basic truth, over against our human world. In professing to make a new beginning in philosophy, to trace our ideas only as they are generated in experience, Locke is operating with loaded dice.

It is not the first, nor is it the last, time that this happens in philosophy. A philosopher professes to make a really fresh start in his discipline, to wipe the board clean and begin with experience as it comes to us, without any constraining assumptions. Alas, he is found to carry in his intellectual baggage assumptions unsuspected by himself, as a consequence of which his data became selective and screened. He cannot see the glasses through which he is seeing. Hence, there is some wisdom in the alternative course that will later be pursued by Kant. Since we are bound to begin with a priori assumptions in any case—the human mind is never, as Locke assumes, that blank tablet on which experience writes—why not begin with a critique of the a priori itself, to try to determine which of our assumptions are necessary and legitimate and which arbitrary and distorting. The success of that effort (by Kant) still remains to be seen.

Meanwhile, the overwhelming historical fact here is that by Locke's time the New Science—modern physics—has taken over the intellectual imagination of the philosophers. It is within or against that background that their thought now has to move. Materialism, of course, is an ancient doctrine; it is a natural way in which the mind moves, or tends to move, when it reflects on the world around us. But there is a world-shaking difference now in the materialism that emerges at the beginning of our period: materialism has now become "scientific"; it seems to have behind it the most compelling body of science that the human mind has yet constructed. But there remains a disturbing disparity here between two worlds. Underneath the human world of our common experience lies the "really real" world of matter in motion: atoms in the void spinning out our destinies. The discrepancy between these two worlds—the world of science and the human world—becomes thus a central and disturbing theme of modern thought and continues unabatedly so into our own time.

And one of the first, and most brilliant, minds to be disturbed by it was Locke's successor among the empiricists, George Berkeley.

THE DEMATERIALIZED WORLD

If we reflect that it took the combined efforts of England, Ireland, and Scotland to produce the great triumvirate of British empiricism—Locke, Berkeley, and Hume—then we may also be grateful, for the sake of variety, that the national traits of each group emerge in the philosophers themselves. Certainly the Irishman George Berkeley (1685?–1753) exhibits qualities which we commonly associate with the Irish: a capacity for poetry and the poetic, a sweeping and sometimes fanciful imagination, and a boldness to plunge into a position that, at first glimpse, might seem utter paradox. On the other side of the coin, he had very acute critical powers. He wrote an important work on Newton's calculus, making some very sharp criticisms of its mathematical concepts that were not to be adequately dealt with until the mathematicians of the nineteenth century. It was these critical and dialectical powers that he was to turn on Locke.

But before we come to the dialectical detail of his arguments, perhaps we should retain for a moment the poetic impact of his thought, for philosophy becomes impoverished without that impact. The poet Yeats, with the fervor that perhaps only one Irishman can command in saluting another, writes:

> And God-appointed Berkeley that proved all
>   things a dream,
> That this pragmatical, preposterous, pig of a world,
> Its farrow that so solid seem
> Must vanish on the instant
> If the mind but change its theme.

If we choose to be literal, Yeats is mistaken here: Berkeley does not prove all things a dream—far from it. No matter; Yeats's beautiful and impassioned lines register the spiritual impact of Berkeley: He is, above all, at least in the acceptance of the general reader, the philosopher of mind, and of the power of mind over matter. The phrase "the power of mind over matter" may seem too vague to some technical philosophers, but it is readily understood and indeed charged with meaning for ordinary people; and philosophy loses much of its vitality if it loses contact with the life of the people. The power of mind over matter! The question of freedom is compressed into that phrase. For if our mind (however you analyze the mind) does not have power at some point over matter and the force of matter, then we are not free. Or consider the emergence of mind within the course of evolution: Mind may be an accidental freak appearing arbitrarily within the world of matter. But suppose the passage from matter to mind is indicative of some significant trend in nature. Then perhaps there is some meaning to this world, and perhaps even a God. Thus the great issues of human freedom and God are implicated with the question of the rival claims of mind and matter. And on this point there is no doubt where Berkeley stands.

Nevertheless, he does not reduce the actual world around us to a dream. On the contrary, he comes forward as its great defender, against Locke. The real world of our common experience contains trees, grass, singing birds; houses and other people; chairs and tables; etc., etc. In our daily life these are evidently and substantially there, and not at all "subjective" appearances of something else; and for Berkeley, too, they are evidently and substantially there. It is Locke who would undermine their reality, and make it secondary to some underlying abstractions of physics. And here Berkeley turns Locke's own empiricist weapons back upon their originator.

Locke had stripped the world of its colors, sounds, odors— the so-called secondary qualities. His argument had been that these qualities were obviously relative to the perceiver and the conditions of his perceiving, and therefore could not be objective. Color, for example, varies with the conditions of light, the eyes of the perceiver, and his distance from the object. Very well, then; if relativity is the great arguing point of Locke, why not give it back to him at full force? Are his precious primary qualities exempt from all reference to the perceiver? What, for example, is *the* shape of an object but a series of perspectives we have of it? And motion and rest, which Locke as a good Newtonian had taken as absolute, are clearly relative to the movement of the perceiver. Here Berkeley introduces the principle of relativity in a bold and thoroughgoing form that was not to emerge again until Einstein in the twentieth century.

The motion or rest of material particles had been taken as absolute by Locke because there was the absolute space of Newton in which they moved or remained at rest. And here Berkeley performs one of his most audacious acts of analysis, as he seeks to pull down one of the sacred pillars of the Newtonian world. Space—the absolute space of Newton, container of all that is—is not given as a reality in and of itself. It is built up as a high-level abstraction from our perceptions of touch and vision. It is derived from experience; it is not the container of experience. We invert the proper order by taking the abstraction as a concrete reality.

In sum, the whole world of matter, which Locke would make the substratum, or underlying reality, for the world of our common experience, is in fact a high-level intellectual construction. It is a case of misplaced concreteness, as the philosopher A. N. Whitehead in our century has called it: the abstract concepts of physics are taken as ultimately concrete in place of the ordinary world of common experience. Berkeley stands with this ordinary world, and he consistently reassures his ordinary reader that he is on his side against the materialism of sophisticated philosophers.

Yet there is a difference, for Berkeley points out that this common world of ours is everywhere permeated by mind, and this is an aspect the ordinary citizen is not usually aware of or chooses to forget. There is no entity—nothing at all—that we can speak of as existing in and of itself apart from some perspective or structure of the mind that grasps it. This is a principle that Immanuel Kant will later take over and build upon; and the triumph of Berkeley's analysis is to have established this principle against materialism. We cannot escape from mind, not even, as in our day, by fleeing to the computer.

Indeed, the computer itself bears witness to the primacy of

the human mind through the whole course of its operations. (We shall have more to say on the subject of computers later, but perhaps a preliminary indication here may serve as a pointer.) In the first place, the computer itself is a tool, a machine, that has been created by the human mind. We may yet design computers that build other computers—as we inhabit more and more a world of robots—but the initial push in the whole process must come from a human mind that plans the whole. But beyond its sheer existence, in its most banal operations the computer bears witness to the presence of mind in the programming of its operations. The machine is perfectly useless in the hands of someone who does not know how to program it. A program is an intelligent design (that is, design initiated by a human intelligence) in accordance with which the machine operates significantly. We speak of "hard facts," and the computer is thought to store these up for us and deal them out when they are needed. But whether the so-called hard facts are significant or relevant depends on some intelligent perspective from which they are organized. We come back always to the presence of mind in the whole process.

Though Berkeley claims persistently that he is speaking in defense of our common, everyday experience, there nevertheless seems to be a snag for the ordinary person when Berkeley encapsulates his whole position in the famous slogan: *"Esse est percipi,* to be is to be perceived." Do objects, then, cease to exist when they are not perceived? When I walk out of this room, do the chairs and tables I am now perceiving go out of existence? Berkeley keeps to his slogan but introduces God as the perceiver who is always there to maintain the constant existence of objects when human perceivers vanish. Here God would seem an unnecessary intrusion into an otherwise cogent analysis of sense perception.

How can Berkeley, the arch-empiricist, more critically empirical about our sense perceptions than Locke, speak so directly about the mind of God? Or about mind at all? He had fired his dialectical buckshot at Locke's notion of matter as being ungrounded in our ordinary sensuous perceptions. But mind, like matter, is not given in sensuous experience; how, then, in all consistency, can he introduce the notion of mind as meaningful? Because, he answers, we have a direct awareness or intuition of our own minds: When we are conscious of anything, we are also conscious that we are conscious. And by analogy, of finite with infinite, we may speak of God as infinite mind. Thus this "notion" of God, though dimly and imperfectly grasped, will nevertheless not be meaningless like Locke's concept of matter, which runs roughshod over the ordinary facts of perception.

Leaving God aside, we come here to a crucial fork in the road, where empiricists now divide. Are we aware of ourselves as minds? The ordinary person would say yes. I am not only aware of the sensory datum—the brown of the table on which I write and the white of the wall opposite—but I am aware of my own consciousness perceiving it. And I am also aware of the I—an ego, a self—that is at the center of this consciousness. And I am aware also that I am the same conscious self as yesterday, however different the sensations I am now bombarded with. But when we pass from the ordinary person to the philosophers, or at least some philosophers, then this primary fact of self-consciousness somehow becomes dubious. Sensations seem such clear and distinct, hard and fast, objective data that consciousness, or mind, by comparison, begins to look like a fleeting and unwarranted ghost. The temptation arises, then, to reduce mind to sensations or a composite of sensations. Accordingly, empiricists were divided between the tender-minded and the tough-minded, as William James later would put it. If the word "empiricism" means an openness and fidelity to experience, then we should not close the gates arbitrarily against any mode of intuition or awareness. But there are those empiricists who, seemingly more "tough-minded" and in pursuit of hard fact, feel compelled to give ultimate priority to sensation only.

We come thus to the figure of David Hume (1711–76), the

third of our empiricist trio, and the archetypal figure of sensationalism. He is thus the final step in the dialectical drama of British empiricism: As Berkeley reduced Locke's material substance to a conglomerate of sense perceptions, so Hume seeks to reduce Berkeley's mind to a heap of sense impressions. We have gone as far here as a certain empiricism can take us—unless perhaps sensations themselves can be reduced to something else.

NEITHER MIND NOR MATTER

From Berkeley to Hume we take a giant step in the progress of the modern mind. We definitely enter the eighteenth century—the Enlightenment, or Age of Reason, as it prided to call itself. The mind of the seventeenth century was firmly planted in God, and Berkeley is, in that respect, a throwback to the earlier century. As a religious man, he believed that we live, move, and have our being in God, and as a philosopher, he carried on his thinking within that presence. But with Hume we enter the secular world of modernity. God has begun to withdraw, and henceforth, though there are various seethings of popular piety, the intellectuals maintain a rather distant relation to the Deity. Hume has neither so profound nor so passionate a mind as to undergo the experience of godlessness as Nietzsche would a century later. As a cool and cautious Scotsman, he preferred to remain on civil, if remote, terms with his Maker.

The secular Age of Reason, however, was not so sedate and sober an affair as its outward bearing might suggest. It was to bring with it some revolutionary thoughts about human society, and it terminates with the violence of the French Revolution, the first truly modern revolution in human history, and the one from which all subsequent revolutionary movements develop. Had he lived long enough to see it, Hume's rather complacent temperament would have been uneasy at all that disturbance. As it turned out, however, he was to produce something almost as revolutionary in his own philosophy.

It happens also to be a philosophy curiously at odds with our ordinary experience of the world. Yet that has seemed no barrier to its popularity with some minds. Hume, indeed, was to become the chosen figure, the foundation of later positivism, and particularly positivism in our century. As they came on the scene in the 1920s and 1930s, deriving from the early work of Wittgenstein, the positivists described their doctrine as "logical positivism," and it consisted mainly of Hume plus the addition of modern mathematical logic. That Hume's account of experience was singularly reductive did not deter them. It looked "exact," and there is a certain type of mind that prefers exactness, or what looks like exactness, to adequacy.

To begin with, Hume reduces experience to a succession of sense impressions, and our world, so he holds is constructed out of this welter of impressions. Moreover, these impressions are atomistic—discrete and disconnected from each other: "I see a colored surface" or "I hear a sound." And then there are impressions of our body: "I feel cold"; or of the emotions: "I feel sad." (We note here, in passing, that feelings and sensations are gathered together under the term "impressions." The confusion of feelings and sensations is one of the cardinal temptations of our civilization.) Our mortal life is a stream of such discrete impressions. But we may immediately observe here that our feeling of sadness is not a discrete datum like the brown of the table. My mood infuses my whole world and penetrates the other impressions I may be receiving. To feel cold and sad is different from feeling sad when the weather is pleasantly warm. It is precisely this relational and interpenetrating aspect of experience that Hume fails to see.

Indeed, it is the atomicity of his world that accounts for Hume's celebrated skeptical doubts about cause and effect, which seem to place the whole edifice of nature on a shaky foundation. Consider two billiard balls, A and B. They are discrete and separate entities. A moves and strikes B, and B moves. We say that A is the cause of B's movement. The more this happens, the more probable, we say, is it that B will move; and when it has happened many times, we even go on to say that B must move. But whence this "must"—this tie of necessity between the two phenomena? We have no distinct impression of any necessary bond between the two. We observe only two discrete entities, this momentary contact ("contiguity in space") and the movement of B that follows ("succession in time"). What justifies us, then, in speaking of causal necessity, or even that the probability of B's movement is increased by each repetition of the whole phenomenon? Hume's answer is abrupt and bleak: There is no logical justification at all; our inference from cause to effect is merely an expression of human habit. We have made the inference in the past, and it worked; and we continue to do so out of the inertia of human habit. Thus the whole edifice of science—that stunning edifice of the New Science, of which Hume's contemporaries stood in such awe—becomes merely a highly formal expression of human habit.

Notice that cause and effect here remain external to each other. Suppose, however, we examine another order of causation equally mundane. Reader, have you ever imbibed too much of sour-mash bourbon, and wakened the next day with the hangover only that particular liquor can give? You will taste, alas, the sour dregs of your drink all through your discomfiture. The cause here does not remain external; it enters into the being of its effect. Or have you ever eaten of a fish stew which by evil chance contained a bad clam? You may end by tasting that bad clam all through the nausea of the next day. The cause here penetrates—oh, how unpleasantly and unmistakenly so!—its sad effect.

Indeed, once we examine how the body is present in and through consciousness, we realize that consciousness, for Hume, is essentially bodiless. Here, he is in the same boat with Descartes, though the consciousness in question is a very different one from Descartes's. The mind sits precariously, externally to its body, from which it receives the discrete data of impressions. It is never a mind embedded in its body.

We come, finally, to the most shocking of Hume's skeptical conclusions: the self, he tells us, is only a heap of perceptions. The I, or ego, suffered here a blow from which the fragmentation of the Modern Age has never rescued it. We live in a world where the flow of sensations, copiously fed to us by all the devices of technology, can virtually turn the ordinary citizen into a heap of perceptions. Others more sensitive, assailed by its complexities, tend to lose their belief in anything like a definite ego. " 'I,' say I. Unbelieving," writes Samuel Beckett at the beginning of *The Unnamable*, a novel that pursues, but to no avail, the fragmentary and fleeing ego. In this respect the work might be taken as a symbol of our whole culture, which in its theoretical part has lost its grip on the self.

It is easy to see the difficulty that leads Hume in this direction. The self is, in its way, uncapturable. I see the brown surface of the table, but I cannot see the see-er, the I that sees. If I go through the jungle of consciousness, the only "hard" data I seem to find are these of sensation. What am I now? I am seeing, hearing, feeling warm or cold, etc. I find nothing but sensory data or the series of past data. The mind, the self, the I, or ego—call it or them what you will—seem to flee like insubstantial ghosts, uncapturable in any sensory experience.

But perhaps Hume is looking in the wrong direction. It is a "categorial mistake"—to use the once fashionable phrase—to expect the self to be exhibited as a sensory datum. As one wit has put it: Hume is like a man who goes outside his house and looks through the window to see if he is at home. It is the error noted earlier: the philosopher's temptation to take a purely spectator view of the mind, forgetting that he himself is a participant. He stands outside the self and looks for it as some kind of sensory datum, forgetting that he himself has launched the search and is involved in it throughout.

Bertrand Russell at one point tried to systematize Hume by adding a bit of modern logic.[1] The self now becomes an aggregate or class of sense data. But Russell, as is his wont, thinks it sufficient to establish a class simply by verbal appellation, without indicating how it is to be constructed—i.e., how its members are to be determined. Suppose, for example, I am nothing but a class of sense data. Very well; but which data? Well, the data *I* am now perceiving. The entity to be defined has to be invoked in its definition. A peculiarly ticklish difficulty arises in the case of memory, which Russell, as a thoroughgoing Humean, seeks to define in terms of sensation. There is my present self, the class of my sense data now, at time t_1; and there is the self of yesterday, the set of data at t_2. Memory is the presence of that earlier set to me now. Here again, the data of yesterday's self are those that I remember now—and we are caught up once more in circularity. Moreover, and perhaps especially, when I remember yesterday's data I am not in the least experiencing them in the way I am now observing the data around me. Remembering a color, no matter how vividly, is a very different thing from seeing the color now before me. Russell's logical language produces a semblance of precision but really leaves things as muddled as they were. It is characteristic of our technical civilization that it tends to proliferate in precise or pseudo-precise language that leaves us more confused about the matters of ordinary life than we would otherwise be. We are on the way to becoming a culture swamped by its own verbalisms.

Questionable and uncertain as it may be, Hume's philosophic doctrine was nevertheless to leave its mark. It seems paradoxical to connect this cool, civilized, and temperate Scotsman with the rabid sensationalism that now affects a good part of our civilization. Sensation is the function of the psyche that takes in facts; and as the thirst for facts, facts, facts takes over the mind, the qualities of feeling and intuition

[1] In *The Analysis of Mind.*

tend to recede; and on the level of personal relations and love, this thirst turns into what one critic has described as the "sensual mania" of our time. Nevertheless, whether as prophecy or cause, Hume points in the direction of what we are now going through.

In any case, simply on the philosophical level, Hume's thought left ravages upon the European mind that his successor Immanuel Kant, the greatest mind of the Enlightenment, felt it incumbent upon himself to repair.

Part II

The Pivot

Four

A Map of the Modern World

IMMANUEL KANT (1724–1804) seems always to evoke a sense of discrepancy between the modesty of his personal figure and the awesome place he was to occupy in the history of thought. Even his diminutive size (he was scarcely five feet high) has been used to point up the contrast. This picture of the little professor, who led such a quiet and well regulated life—so precisely regulated, indeed, that the townspeople of Königsberg were said to set their watches by his daily walk—and yet whose thinking had such vast consequences, has become a permanent fixture of our general historical imagination. The poet Heinrich Heine compares him, rather sensationally, to Robespierre, also a modest figure, who brought in the Reign of Terror and destroyed the *ancien régime.* So Kant laid waste the traditional arguments for God and undermined

theology. The good citizens of Königsberg would have regarded him differently if they had known the thoughts he was
harboring.

Today we might put the emphasis another way. The destructive consequences of his thought are certainly there, but
what strikes us more is that he is the last great thinker in
whom the intellectual unity of the Western mind is still held
together. Thereafter that unity was to fall apart, diverge in a
number of irreconcilable directions, become fragmented. It is
still the unity of a fundamentally theistic civilization that is
preserved in Kant's system. His thought, in all the major divisions of philosophy, always ends with God. Yet this unity is a
precarious one, more precarious than Kant himself could
imagine. He sat securely within the piety of his place and
time, but he had in fact departed farther from God than he
realized.

Kant called his philosophy the "critical philosophy." He
wished thereby to separate himself from the dogmatism of
some of his great predecessors—the dogmatism of speculative
metaphysics and theology in Leibnitz, on the one hand, and
the dogmatic skepticism of Hume on the other. The skeptical
naysayer can be as uncritical as the most rampant believer—a
fact which some of our contemporaries now seem to forget.
Kant insists everywhere on the limits and conditions under
which the mind must operate—but these happen also to be
the conditions under which it operates effectively and produc-
tively. Even in matters of religion and God—perhaps most of
all there—we have to be aware of the limitations with which
our human nature is hedged about. The eighteenth century, in
comparison with the seventeenth, is indeed a critical age—the
so-called Age of Reason; and Kant's philosophy is its deepest
philosophical voice. The bourgeois has now entered history,
and his voice is one of sobriety, prudence, caution.

Thus, though Kant's greatness is certainly due to his own
powers of mind, just as surely his significance would not be
what it is if he had not appeared at the particular juncture of

history when he did. He comes upon the scene at the end of the first great wave of our Modern Age, and he helps to launch the second wave (in the midst of which we still are). Thus he has before him the thought of his great modern predecessors. They had raised problems which are crucial to this epoch that humankind has now entered, and Kant is in a position to sift out and reflect upon the opposed answers they give. His genius is, above all, reflective. He does not strike us as having the eruptive and innovating brilliance of a Descartes or a Leibnitz. But if he builds upon what others have thought, sifting through their positions and seeing beyond them, his results are nonetheless startling for that. And he had some very great predecessors to pore over.

Also, he had before him the body of the "New Science," modern science, in rounded and recognizable shape. His great predecessors, such as Descartes and Leibnitz, had been in the midst of creating it; Kant, at the end of the eighteenth century, has the whole edifice before his eyes, and is at a sufficient distance to reflect upon it. And, once again, his genius is for reflection: he is the first thinker who arrives at a really philosophical comprehension of what modern science is and means. And, we may add, it is an understanding of science at a level or depth that is not reached again until Heidegger in our own time.

Some idea of his unique historical position may be conveyed by the accompanying diagram. The picture we draw claims no originality for itself. It is the kind of diagram we might draw in a classroom, and the reader may take it as a mere pedagogical device. But if one contemplates it at length, certain ideas emerge. Whatever depth or originality we can take from it derives from the originality of the reflections we bring to it.

In the first place, then, why do we call this "A Map of the Modern World"? Is that title merely a colorful toy, a piece of journalistic bravado? Not at all. It expresses our conviction that the fundamental history of humankind is the history of mind. The human race is unique among the animal species in that it has a history, and it has a history only because it has a peculiar organ, the mind, which is able to generate new thoughts and theories, new forms of being, new rites and religions, and new schemes for managing social and political life. Without these transformations of the life of the mind, there would be no history to relate, no story to tell—only the bare chronicles of repetition.

A MAP OF THE MODERN WORLD: I

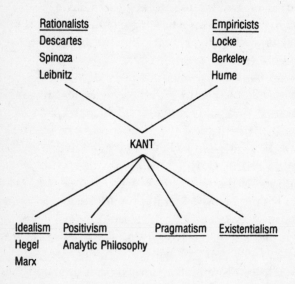

Our view is not the one currently in vogue among academic historians. The trend now is for "social history"—the minute documentation of the material facts of social life. No doubt, such history is necessary and useful, but it can never give us the full human significance of the data it records. It cannot even explain the historical fact that it is so touted nowadays: one of its attractions is that it appears "more scientific," but that view is itself a philosophical predilection on the part of its practitioners, and thus the projection of a certain cast of mind. Nor can this grubby factual history grasp the great initiating forces in history, which are usually in the form of ideas and ideologies. We come back thus always to the human mind at the center of its own history.

But why philosophy at that center? Even if we grant that the human mind sits, like a spider, at the center of its history, why should philosophy, and the contending schools of philosophy, be given such a featured role in our impromptu little chart, which claims—no less!—to be a map of the modern world? Our answer is the plain and traditional one: because philosophy is the effort of our human mind to know itself and take stock of the universe and our place in it. The question, and the doubt it reflects, are prompted, I suspect, by the narrow and restricted place that philosophy now holds in our culture. It is a small department within the university, and the philosophers engaged in it talk mostly with each other, and only rarely if at all to the general public. But that in itself is an indication of the place of spirit in a particular epoch. If a culture is able to produce only one philosophy—positivism, say—this does not mean that our citizens go around deliberately spouting positivist principles. Positivism simply inhabits their spirit in the absence of any other, contravening doctrine. Similarly with the diversity of philosophic schools in any period; that may be a sign of intellectual cleverness and richness, or of a scattering and confusion of spirit; and we have to look carefully to see which. A time shows itself by what it has produced—particularly by what it has produced in the way of thinking, and specifically, thinking about the most fundamental conditions of our own, human existence.

Another question immediately arises as to whether a philosophy merely "reflects" its time or whether it is causally efficacious and generates consequences in the general life of society. (This is a variant of our persistent question whether mind is essentially active or passive.) The question would seem to be based on a somewhat artificial misconception of how mind actually works within a society. The life of the mind pervades a society even on its most routine and ordinary levels. And if some of that life happens to rise to theoretical expression in a philosophy, this is not a mere passive "reflection" of something already there and fully formed. On the contrary, in giving form and shape to attitudes present in a more inchoate fashion, it *projects* the future. The important philosophers, those who really have vision, shape the mind and consequently the social life of the future. We would not be where we are now without them. The whole of the present book, we trust, may provide some demonstration of that contention.

There is, of course, something humanly deeper than philosophy—and that is religion. Though our little chart does not name it, religion enters into our picture, because the philosophies of our modern epoch—of the so-called "death of God" —have had continuously to traffic with the religious issue, if sometimes mainly by way of separating themselves from all ties with religion. The religious question is ultimately at the center of all philosophy, even if it be by way of rejection. That some contemporary philosophers have reached the point where they never enter into the question, where the philosopher never seems even to be troubled by the word "God," is itself a profound sign of the state of our culture. It took an immense amount of philosophic thinking and unthinking to prepare the human psyche for this matter-of-fact state of godlessness. Perhaps it is a harbinger of the future at which the human species—all of us—will someday arrive. But perhaps not; and certainly not yet.

There is also the activity of art, which captures a kind of truth, of which philosophy may take note but which it cannot produce of itself. Our little map does not mean to exclude this vision of art. It is part of the background from which we see the sequence of modern philosophies, and we shall make use of it. Perhaps modern art tells us most, if we have but eyes to see, about the nature of the modern age which we have traversed or which has almost finished us. But here we confine ourselves to philosophy, to use explicit intellectual expression of the human mind about itself and its possible destiny. It is a matter of focus.

Yet there is one strictly philosophical omission from our chart that we have now to repair. Curiously enough, it is not a philosophy represented by any distinct philosopher or school; it is an element that circulates among all of them, more often than not as an element to be absorbed and transcended or else fought against and rejected. We refer, of course, to *scientific materialism*, the pervasive current that flows around all modern philosophizing. That materialism need not be explicitly professed as a creed; it becomes the *de facto* philosophy of an era reaping great triumphs in the physical sciences and in technology and pushing more and more of its energies into those fields. The achievements in the physical sciences and technology become the invisible standard—and sometimes not altogether invisible—by which to measure thinking in all domains. The discoveries in physics and chemistry, the amazing proliferation of machines and apparatus, seem somehow solid and real; and in comparison with these, any meditation about matters like the human soul are bound to seem ghostly, insubstantial.

Accordingly, we have to amend our little chart in the style of those old-fashioned maps that represented the currents of ocean surrounding the isolated land masses. As the flow of the ocean molds the contours of land, so this current of materialism shapes the actual life of our time. However we may hide from it in our philosophic study, we are caught in its flow as soon as we step outside into the actual world. If our culture is to take a new turn, and resolve some of its most troubling questions, it will only be when, at long last, it is able to come to philosophic terms with this scientific materialism.

We come back now to Kant. Our map represents gathering and dispersion, and in this general rhythm it is accurate: the movement of modernity has been one of spiritual dispersion. But it would be a mistake to think that the philosophies which followed Kant took over and assimilated the full body of his

A MAP OF THE MODERN WORLD: II

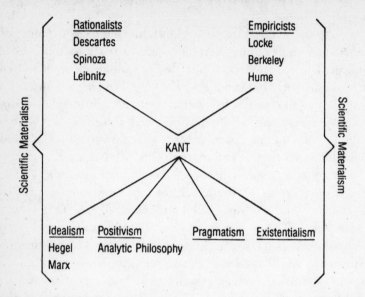

thought, therefore preserving it for us. On the contrary, Kant is one of the great thinkers whose real intent has virtually been forgotten by us today. We have to enter his thought to retrieve it. The surface of his thought is deceptive: the imposing façade of terminology leads one to believe that his thinking is closed and fixed. When we enter that thought, and try to think it from within, we find that it is far more open and exploratory than we had imagined; that it is, like the thought of all the greatest philosophers, unfinished. We shall also find that it is absolutely contemporary—in the sense in which all genuine philosophy is eternally contemporary.

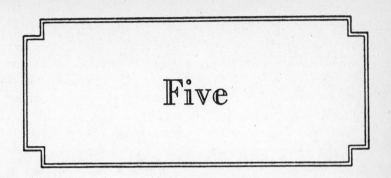

Five

The Power of Mind

CAN MIND BE REDUCED TO MATTER? This has been a common and terse way of putting the question of materialism. The materialist, then, would be someone who answers this question in the affirmative: the ultimate constituents of the world are bits of matter in motion, and what we call mind is really the outcome of such forces. This may seem clear, but it is largely a piece of sweeping rhetoric. Indeed, it is doubtful whether the question itself, put in this common form, can be given any precise or determinable meaning: It becomes a "metaphysical" question in the bad sense of this word, about which some contemporary philosophers have so copiously instructed us.

We have therefore to change our tack and ask a different question. If we ask whether the mind can and does play an active role in our human life or whether it is merely passive and receptive, then our question remains within the confines of experience. It becomes, to use the philosophical lingo, "phenomenological," rather than "metaphysical." Our answer will nonetheless effectively draw the teeth of materialism. For if mind does have an essentially active and organizing role in our experience, the materialist contention, in its practical bearings at least, ceases to have much force.

That is why Kant is chosen here as the next major figure in this drama of mind that we are sketching. No other philosopher has brought forward more effectively than he this active and organizing role of mind within our human experience. He thus becomes a central figure in our story. And it will be worthwhile following his message carefully, transposing it wherever we can into our more ordinary language.

The British empiricists (from Locke through Hume) had abounded in expressions of the mind's passivity, "Ideas are *imprinted* upon the mind"; "The mind is a blank tablet on which experience writes." Etc., etc. But if you turn to experience, you find that the mind appears to *do* much more than these philosophers would give it credit for. You are sitting, say, at dinner with five or six people and you observe the way in which the conversation moves around from person to person. Each person takes in the situation and takes up the drift of the conversation differently, and then pushes it in his or her direction. The experience of "taking in" any situation is highly selective and organizing. You do not receive an imprint on the mind as a photographic plate receives an impression. You pick and choose, and above all, in "taking in" the situation, you perceive a direction in which it may be headed. Your perception points toward a possible future that events may take, which is not given in any purely passive reception.

Suppose we turn this suggestion now to one of the most significant actions in the history of our species: the construction of numbers. Do not be frightened, reader, at the mention of anything mathematical. We shall not go beyond the level of the most elementary mathematics—indeed, we shall be at the basement level that lies below the arithmetic you learned in elementary school.

Perhaps, however, one further word of reassurance is due the reader here. The subject of mathematics, as we shall discuss it, is not a departure from our main theme, which happens to be the power of the human mind. Mathematics is one of the clearest and most shining examples of this power of the mind to bring order into our experience. We all participate in it, even on the most elementary level, in the fact that we keep dates and reckon up our bills; and we should reflect a little on the significance of what we are doing when we perform these elementary operations. At the present time, our popular culture tends to be swamped by images of the psychopathology of human reason. As the lingo of psychoanalysis and psychotherapy have spread and become bastardized, reason tends to be looked at as a faculty of distortion and concealment—the instrument by which we build elaborate structures by which to hide from the truth of our emotions. No doubt, there is a truth here, but it is not the whole truth about human reason. Perhaps, then, mathematics may serve as a needed countervailing example of the legitimate powers of reason, and we all should reflect a little about it. In particular, we need to reflect on the basic operations of mind as it builds mathematics.

Accordingly, with Kant at our shoulder, we have now to conceive the procedure by which the human mind originally constructed numbers.

We know from anthropology that there were primitive cultures that had only a most rudimentary conception of the number system. Their counting consisted of one, two, three, and then just "many." However sharp as sensory observers of their environment, they had not made the effort of concentration to build a numbering system. Pushing back a little, we may imagine a time when the animal that is classified biologically as *Homo sapiens* was as yet so culturally low in his mental development that he did not yet have even the most elementary conceptions of number and numbers. In short, we are thinking of a time when numbers did not exist.

That is a situation that ought to give philosophers of mathematics pause. Shall we say that numbers nevertheless subsisted in some Platonic heaven waiting to be plucked down by some Promethean mind? Here we move into the realm of myths, of which twenty-five hundred years of philosophic wrangling have failed to supply any workable meaning. In any case, that supposed Prometheus would have to go through the Kantian operations of constructing the numbers.

Or suppose we look the other way: toward the future. If, after some unimaginable disaster, the human species should relapse into a primeval stupor, it is conceivable that mathematics would be forgotten. (We know now, from our reading of Heidegger, that forgetting is also one of the capacities of the human mind.) Suppose, however, that the textbooks of mathematics have somehow survived; there they are, row upon row, in the shelves of the library, and those future beings point at them: "That's mathematics," remembering the name but not understanding the least thing that is in those books. Assuredly "that" is not mathematics, for mathematics has ceased to exist, since there are no human beings who understand it. It is well to remember such a dire possibility against one current philosophy of mathematics that holds mathematics deals simply with marks on paper. In fact, the marks on paper are mathematical only if there are minds able to give them a mathematical meaning.

We come back now to the primal situation in which numbers were constructed by some early group of our human species. In its external features our account will be fanciful, but in its formal features—its "transcendental" structure, as Kant would say—the procedure must have gone this way, whatever the external circumstances were.

We are in a cave, Plato's cave if you will. Someone, the chief of the tribe, announces, "Today the sun rose, and I am going to scratch a mark on this side of the wall. Tomorrow when it rises again and the light fills our heaven, I will make another mark, and so for each day afterward." And so a series begins to take shape on the wall:

$$| \quad | \quad | \quad | \quad | \ . \ . \ .$$

Bit by bit, as the marks gather, we notice the place of each in the sequence and give each one its name, its number-name; and so the birth of number begins to take place for the human species.

Let us pause to reflect on what has taken place here. The mind has directed its attention to the future ("Tomorrow when [the sun] rises"), and then on the morrow puts together the present with the past. The activity of mind here is a synthesis (synthesis, from the Greek, is literally a putting together of two things). The words "synthesis" and "synthetic" are central and frequent in the Kantian text, and they sometimes come in for elaborate discussion. But we should never forget the simple idea that lies at the root of these words: the putting together of disparate things into some significant unity or pattern.

Notice that this is a different kind of joining than modern psychology is likely to emphasize. We today are obsessed with the notion of the conditioned response. A stimulus occurs and we respond; and if the two are repeated often enough, we end by associating them in our mind. The bell rings, and dinner is brought to the dog; in time, he will end by salivating when he hears the sound of the bell. And we take this as a fundamental model of the human mind. No doubt, it is a model that applies to a good deal of our experience, but it is hardly complete, and it does not apply to the particular case we are dealing with here. We are talking about a synthesis by the mind in view of some planned end or structure, and which in fact does bring a new structure and meaning into existence. In short, we are talking about an active, rather than a passive, operation of mind.

Now, to come back to our primitive example of counting:

there must be a continuity of consciousness persisting from today to tomorrow in order to gather the two together and make a fresh mark on the wall. More than this: consciousness is not just a blank consciousness; it has an I, an ego, accompanying it. The I that makes the mark today must in some sense be the same I that placed a mark yesterday and will place yet another mark tomorrow—otherwise the whole operation falls apart. "In some sense," but what sense? Ah, that is the nub of the whole question about the human soul as we are and shall be dealing with it throughout. Kant here is the sober and cautious critical philosopher, and he hedges his answer. How much of the ego persists from today to tomorrow? Only as much, he tells us, as is required to give continuity and meaning to the particular process of thought—in short, a formal, or, in the Kantian terminology, a transcendental, ego.

Kant has here taken a decisive step beyond Hume, but perhaps has not gone quite as far as he might. Certainly, the Humean conception of the ego as a momentary heap of impressions or perceptions here collapses. A self that is only a heap of impressions could not count up to five. It would not have the continuity of consciousness required to do so; nor could it have the center of consciousness, the ego, that can direct attention to the future and then gather it together with the past (a passive heap of impressions cannot project toward the future).

But does Kant here give us the concrete ego—the actually existing self that each of us in that imaginary cave would have been while the process of counting went on from day to day? Hardly. In fact, he turns most of his polemic against traditional theological thought that had tried to argue that this I accompanying consciousness is a pure, immaterial substance (and thus possibly immortal). In this respect Kant is a good Humean carrying out the critical thrust of Hume's philosophy. In fact, he is—at least in this respect—a more rigorous Humean than Hume himself.

Yet, even within the confines of his own thought, Kant

could have given a place to this concrete self more adequately than he has. We shall return to this issue shortly.

MATHEMATICS AND LOGIC; SYNTHETIC AND ANALYTIC

Starting with this primary—we might almost say primitive —example of the human mind constructing numbers, we may follow Kant into the larger subject of mathematics generally. And here Kant has a fundamental insight that goes beyond earlier philosophers and yet, sadly, has largely been lost to philosophers today, especially in the Anglo-American world. The insight is this: that mathematics is essentially constructive. Not only does it deal with entities that are constructed by the human mind—there are no numbers, points, straight lines, etc., in nature—but its methods of thought are constructive throughout. It does not proceed by merely substituting one set of symbols for an equivalent set, but by constructing new cases or mathematical entities that bring forward the property under investigation. The geometrician draws lines; the arithmetician builds up a new numerical complex or entity. If he has to prove there is no last prime number, he does so not by contemplating the meaning or essence of "prime" or "number," but by actually constructing a "last" prime and showing it leads to a contradiction.

Kant's view of mathematics is essentially connected with his distinction between the *analytic* and the *synthetic* employment of the human understanding. An analytic proposition, he tells us, is one in which the predicate adds nothing to the subject. "A bald man is a man" does not add to our knowledge. The predicate merely explicates what is already contained in the subject. The sentence is, in modern parlance, a tautology. A synthetic proposition, on the other hand, adds to our knowledge. "Man is an animal with a bivalvular heart" tells us something we might not have known before.

Kant's distinction has come into much controversy in our period. In the first place, he is chained to the older logic of subject and predicate, and his distinction does not seem rigorous enough to us as practitioners of modern mathematical logic. To speak of a predicate "contained" in its subject seems too vague, psychological, or metaphysical to us. But here, as elsewhere in Kant, his insight may exceed his formulation; and where the details of his formulation are inadequate, it is nevertheless worthwhile to try to see what he was after. In the present case, what he was struggling to get at is a matter of some scope and significance.

Consider the activity of mathematics as it is embodied in the publications of our mathematicians. Some of these papers, we say, are trivial, some significant. What do we mean when we say certain mathematical results are "trivial"? I once complimented a young mathematician, a colleague and friend, on his handing me an offprint of his first published paper. He shrugged modestly: it was trivial, he said, he had not produced anything really new, but merely produced some simplifications in an already known and important proof. In the same vein, we can sift through the history of mathematics and sort out results and achievements of major importance against the trivial efforts of lesser mathematicians. What makes a given theorem in mathematics significant? Because, we say, it really adds something new to our knowledge; it makes us see the mathematical phenomena in a new way. For centuries, from the Greeks and Arabs through the modern Europeans, geometers had striven to square the circle. Then, in the nineteenth century, in 1861, the solution of that age-old problem was definitely proved impossible. That was new knowledge.

Mathematicians regularly speak of "trivial," "significant," and "really new" results. Such words belong to the practical, everyday language of their mathematical world. They are readily understandable and in no way obscure or questionable. They seem to become obscure only in the views of some modern philosophers of logic.

Bertrand Russell, for example, seeks to reduce all of mathematics to logic. Now, the propositions of logic are analytic; i.e., they are tautological and simply say A is A in one form or another. Hence, all of mathematics would also become tautological, though in quite elaborate form. What would it mean, then, to speak of one theorem as "trivial" or another as really "significant"? As tautologies that say A is A, they would all be on the same level.

Russell, never at a loss for words, finds no difficulty in this question. The reasons mathematicians can produce results that surprise us is that we do not see at once the consequences of our own language until they are brought out by logical inference. But those consequences are already there—tautologously there—though we cannot see them all at once. And Russell pushes the point to its metaphysical finale: The reason we cannot see them immediately is that our intellect is finite. An infinite intellect, Russell tells us, would see mathematics immediately for what it is: one single vast tautology.

This is surely a curious tack in interpretation for a positivistically inclined philosopher to take. And we note that A. J. Ayer, in his most sweepingly positivist phase, repeats Russell's point. It is surely strange that the model that a positivist would invoke for understanding mathematics should be so thoroughly nonempirical an entity as an infinite mind! (Should we call it God's?) Do we understand at all what an infinite mind would be?

Here Kant, the shrewd and down-to-earth critical philosopher, comes to our aid: Our human mind is radically finite, and cannot see except from the framework of that finitude. We cannot have any adequate *concept* of an infinite mind, only, at best, a vague and numinous *idea*—certainly nothing we can use as a scientific model for understanding mathematics. It is this same finite mind that produces mathematics by constant inventions and constructions. Did the calculus flow tautologously from previous mathematical language, or was it a new invention: the construction of the idea of a limit?

Kant cites history for confirmation. Logic since Aristotle, he tells us, has made no new discoveries; it has restated and polished the language, but the body of logic remains substantially what it was in Aristotle. Mathematics, on the other hand, has been ceaselessly productive of new discoveries, and never more so than in the two centuries—the seventeenth and the eighteenth—that launched our Modern Age. The particular passage is a famous one in Kant, but Russell jeers: Kant was simply ignorant of modern logic. Russell is both right and wrong here. Kant was certainly historically limited by his time and knew nothing about modern logic. But if he were resurrected, he would find no difficulty in assimilating modern logic to his general view and indeed finding confirmation there. Modern logic has been productive of some new and surprising results because it is *mathematical* logic. The use of a systematic symbolic notation has permitted forms of constructivity not accessible to the older logic. Thus symbols may be numbered, and the resources of arithmetic, ingeniously used, issue in the famous Gödel theorem. Without the connivance of arithmetic, the proof could not be made.

The proof, in fact, turns on an ingenious means that Gödel constructs for numbering the expressions of a language. We then form the proposition: "Statement number X is not provable." When we calculate "number X," we find out that it is the number of the statement itself. Thus the statement says that it itself is not provable. What follows? Well, if a proof should ever happen to turn up, the language would contain a contradiction: The unprovable statement would have been proved. Arithmetic would then be inconsistent. Hence, if arithmetic is indeed consistent, it will be incomplete—that is, will contain some unprovable statements (like this particular statement we have constructed). Obviously, the whole argument can take place only through the constructive device of numbering the expressions of the language.

Yet textbooks in logic and teachers of logic usually fail to convey this point. The usual textbook, after preliminary instruction in the elements of the logical calculus, presents twenty or thirty simple "theorems." The latter are merely symbolic reformulations of the axioms, the proof is made by substitutions of equivalent expressions. But then the text breaks off and there is an indication of theorems of a quite different kind—the Lowenheim-Skolem theorem, for example, or the two Gödel theorems. The sense of these latter is usually conveyed, and sometimes an indication is given of the reasoning behind them. But what is usually lacking is any indication that these are theorems of a very different order from those obtained by mechanical substitution. They are constructive in their procedure, and accordingly of a significance and import beyond the mechanical sample "theorems." They produced new and surprising knowledge. One logician, J. Van Heijenoort, even refers to the Lowenheim-Skolem theorem as "disturbing." Would one ever use such a term for the mechanical samples of "theorems" put forward for pedagogical purposes?

Kant is also historically limited in his attachment to Euclidean geometry. That he came before non-Euclidean geometry had been constructed is a fact of historical contingency, but his philosophy of mathematics exceeds this limitation of personal history. The Kantian view of mathematics can embrace non-Euclidean geometries quite readily. If mathematics deals with certain free constructions of the human mind, and if it is characteristic of this mind to be active, rather than passive, such that its constructions outrun experience, then we should expect the invention of non-Euclidean geometries that are not confined to our habitual perceptions of space. Thus Kant's attachment to Euclidean geometry, which is often cited to discredit his philosophy of mathematics, is not at all essential to that philosophy.

To some readers, these questions of mathematics and logic may seem rather minute and special in comparison with the larger themes of this book. On the contrary, these questions, though in a way technical, are tied in with broader aspects of our present civilization. For example, it is something of a scandal that our present understanding of the foundations of mathematics is thoroughly unsettled, and the field is contested by rival factions who, in the words of one great modern mathematician, Poincaré (1854–1912), do not really communicate with each other. A culture suffering from such dissension would seem to be in a curious state of fragmentation generally. If we are unclear about our elementary mathematical notions, if we are no longer sure what mathematics is or is about, that would seem to argue a confusion farther along the line. We have built an immense symbolic and verbal structure on obscure foundations. And this condition probably accounts for the immense proliferation of sheer verbalism that infests our culture—and in all fields.

In this respect Kant could be a profitable guide, reminding us that thinking, if it is not to be empty or inflated verbalism, must always be aware of the elementary intuitions from which it starts.

MODERN SCIENCE

As an example of the constructive power of the mind, nothing is more dazzling than the whole edifice of modern science itself. And on the nature of this science Kant provides us with a revolutionary insight, whose profundity we are just beginning to grasp.

The seventeenth century, which created modern science, was not unaware of the revolution it was introducing. Men like Galileo—who called it "the New Science" even while he was in the process of launching it—were militantly conscious that it was a break with the past, that it introduced a way of thinking unknown to the ancients, however wise and subtle they had been; indeed that it was what we might call today a mutation of the human mind.

Kant came a century after the great founders of the New Science. He had been a diligent apprentice of this science in his youth, and continued unceasingly thereafter to reflect upon its meanings. Moreover, where great forerunners like Descartes and Galileo were talking about something that existed largely as their own *project*, by Kant's time this New Science had come fully into existence and had already given a stable and awesome body of knowledge to the world. We may take Kant, then, in a single quotation from the Preface to the Second Edition of his *Critique of Pure Reason*, which appeared in 1786, almost one hundred years after the publication of Newton's *Principia*:

When Galileo caused balls, the weights of which he had himself previously determined, to roll down an inclined plane; when Torricelli made the air carry a weight which he had calculated beforehand to be equal to a definite column of water . . . a light broke upon all students of nature. They learned that reason has insight only into that which it produces after a plan of its own, and that it must not allow itself to be kept, as it were, in nature's leading-strings, but must itself show the way with principles of judgment based upon fixed laws, constraining nature to give answer to questions of reason's own determining . . . Reason, holding in one hand its principles, according to which alone concordant appearances can be admitted as equivalent to laws, and in the other hand the experiment which it has devised in conformity with these principles, must approach nature in order to be taught by it. It must not, however, do so in the character of a pupil who listens to everything that the teacher chooses to say, but of an appointed judge who compels the witness to answer questions which he has himself formulated. Even physics, therefore, owes the beneficent revolution in its point of view entirely to the happy thought, that while reason must seek in nature, not fictitiously ascribe to it, whatever as not being knowable through reason's own resources has to be learnt, if learnt at all, only from nature, it must adopt as its guide, in so seeking, that which it has itself put into nature. It is thus that the study of nature has entered on the secure path of a science after having for so many centuries been nothing but a process of merely random groping.

What Kant is pointing to here is an intrinsic relation between science and technology. The scientist's mind is not a passive mirror that reflects the facts as they are in themselves (whatever that might mean); the scientist constructs models, which are not found among the things given him in his experience, and proceeds to impose those models upon nature. And he must often construct those models conceptually before they are translated at any point into the material constructions of his apparatus in the laboratory.

In this connection, indeed, Kant could have used a simpler and more radical example from Galileo than the famous experiment of the inclined plane, and that is Galileo's very construction of the concept of inertia itself. That concept had thitherto been lacking to the investigators of nature, and the science of mechanics (which was in fact basic to the whole of the New Science) could not get under way without it. What does Galileo do? He does not record passively the facts around him; instead, he constructs a concept that is not precisely found in nature, and indeed is contrary in certain respects to what we find there. Imagine, he tells us, a body on a perfectly frictionless plane; if motion is imparted to this body, it will move on infinitely in a straight line unless its course is impeded or altered by some countervailing force. Well, nature does not present us with any perfectly frictionless planes, or with any plane that is actually infinite in extension. What the concept constructs is a model that is actually contrafactual in the light of our ordinary experience. No matter; it serves as an ideal standard in approximation to which actual situations may be effectively calculated. Here the basic concept of the science, since it is man-made and does not literally copy any single fact in nature, is a product of human artifice and therefore a technical construct as fully as any material piece of apparatus. Here science is technological at its very source, in the formation of basic concepts, and not subsequently and as if by happenstance in the practical applications it may find. The hyphen in the compound expression "science-technology" does not signify the compounding of two independent entities only externally related; it expresses a single historical reality of which the two names denote merely differing aspects.

And this intimate association of the technological and the scientific, which indeed begins at the root, spreads through every branch and leaf of the whole tree. The more advanced and developed a science becomes, the closer its alliance becomes with its own technology and the more closely interwoven part becomes with part in the unity of the whole. One cannot say, antecedently, that any particular fact within the scientific structure, no matter how isolated it may appear at first glance, cannot have an unexpected and surprising connection with some other parts within the whole. The surprising discoveries of such connections, where they had not been at first even suspected, has been a constant and recurring feature of science in its actual development. And so too with any particular technical device, no matter how isolated and particularized for its own small function it may appear: One cannot say of such a device with antecedent certainty that it, or the principle of its operation, will not find an indispensable use elsewhere.

One cannot arbitrarily cut off one part of one's technology and be confident that the whole structure will go on intact and unchanged. In short, once one has grasped the unitary phenomenon that is science-technology, one realizes that it is a single human *project*, and the project moreover under which the history of the past three and a half centuries, the history of our modern epoch, has been and is being played out.

Let us not underestimate the daring and depth of that project. It marks, as Kant notes, a turn in human reason, and consequently a transformation of our human being in its deepest attitudes toward the world. *Humankind turned away from a passive, to a more active, role in its struggle with nature.* Life is given us to be mastered, not as something to drift along with.

Notice some of the key words Kant uses: Man *imposes* his models upon nature; he *compels* nature to answer his questions; he does not merely submit, but seeks a position of *command.* These are words of power, and Kant knew very well what he was about in employing them. He had been a diligent and admiring reader of Francis Bacon, and he was very well aware of Bacon's famous dictum "Knowledge is power." (Bacon, of course, went beyond this sensible maxim to the more violent metaphor "We must put nature to the rack"; and this immediately raises the questionable aspects of our assumption of power over nature, which we shall come to very shortly, in Section III.) Kant internalizes and deepens Bacon's point: Knowledge not only is power in that it may provide us with the instruments to deal with a particular situation; more profoundly still, the step toward knowledge is in its very essence a step toward power. In the very constructivity of our scientific concepts—the human mind fabricates concepts that literally are not found in its ordinary world—we already have taken a step *beyond* nature, in order subsequently to deal with it. Nor is there anything "unnatural" in this step; indeed, in taking that step the human mind comes into the fullness of its own nature and its powers. "God helps those who help themselves," runs the old adage; we have to use all of ourselves—including that part of ourselves that steps beyond nature—in the struggle to cope with nature for the survival of our species.

Thus the project of science-technology, with which the seventeenth century launched our Modern Age, represents, I believe, a genuine and positive transformation of our human being. With it, the doors of knowledge were flung open. In three and a half short centuries, we have come to know more about the nature of the world in which we live than in all the millennia of human history that preceded. And we are only at a beginning, still wrapped in the toils of ignorance. The scientific revolution also created an openness toward the future in another area: in the expectation of social advance, progress, and the radical possibilities of improvement of our human lot upon this earth. Reformers became more hopeful, optimistic, and in some cases, alas, even utopian.

Today, to a great extent, those hopes and that optimism have retreated; and in many quarters, indeed, there prevail a certain despair, passivity, and nihilism toward the future. There is doubt that the future is bound to move upward and onward.

Where, then, does the argument of this chapter lead us? We note the extraordinary power and constructivity of the human mind in producing the great edifice of modern science. And yet, precisely here occurs one of the supreme ironies of modern history: The structure that most emphatically exhibits the power of mind nevertheless leads to the denigration of the human mind. The success of the physical sciences leads to the attitude of scientific materialism, according to which the mind becomes, in one way or another, merely the passive plaything of material forces. The offspring turns against its parent. We forget what we should have learned from Kant: that the imprint of mind is everywhere on the body of this science, and without the founding power of mind it would not exist.

The irony here is not one that we can merely sit back and enjoy aesthetically. This doubt of the mind, in its actual consequences, in the lives of individuals and societies, provides one of the ordeals that modern civilization will have to go through.

From this glimpse of the power of the human mind, we have now to turn to the countervailing feature: its limitations and finitude—features that are also brought out most sharply by Kant.

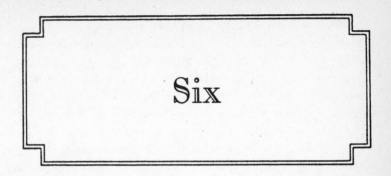

Six

The Finitude of Mind

IT WOULD SEEM an easy matter to grasp our human finitude. We are born at a certain time, live our allotted years, and then are no more. All too plainly and painfully, we are finite creatures of time. And in space, too, however busily we may move about, we cover but a tiny portion of the world. Our ingenious species has now traveled to the moon. But what is the distance to the moon, but the tiniest bubble in the ocean of our galaxy, which in turn is but a bubble in the vastness of space that engulfs it? We seem, thus, to understand our limitations all too well when it comes to space and time.

But such understanding is largely quantitative. We live only so long . . . and no longer. We go so far in space . . . and no farther. Our finitude consists in the limited quantity of space and time that we traverse. True, of course. But the human finitude that Kant would bring before us is of a different sort. It is, so to speak, a qualitative finitude, for it consists in the fact that our human mind is so constituted in its ways of understanding that it cannot grasp conceptually those matters that are of ultimate significance and concern to it.

This mode of our finitude is an uncanny fact about our human nature, and one that we must bring ourselves to reflect on again and again if we are really to see how far it penetrates.

Of course, we commonly bandy the words "finite" and "infinite" around as if they were readily understandable. What is the infinite? Well, we say, it is not finite; and we suppose that this negative verbal formula is enough to give us its meaning. But how is this meaning to be brought before the mind? Suppose, for example, we were to advance, merely as a hypothesis, the proposition that space is actually infinite. What does this "actual infinite" mean? How can we represent its meaning to ourselves? We imagine the following: In a large space capsule we are shot off into space traveling at a speed far beyond our present capacity. The capsule is equipped to maintain human life from generation to generation so that the time of our voyage shall not be circumscribed. We travel far, at an incredible speed, onward and onward through space; the generations come and go, and after five hundred years we ask: "How near have we gotten to the end? How close are we to the edge?" The answer is, No closer. So far as actually getting to the end is concerned, we have come, in a sense, no farther than where we began.

Thus the meaning of the infinite can be grasped by our finite minds only as a *process* to which there is no last term, no end.

The fundamental point of Kant here is his understanding of what a legitimate or meaningful concept is. For a concept to have meaning, we must be able to represent it, directly or indirectly, through some concrete intuition or intuitions. More simply and perhaps crudely: we have to be able to make some kind of mental picture of the concept. Otherwise our thinking becomes empty, and the words we use merely empty verbalisms. (The absence of such intuitions behind much of the chitchat of pseudo-intellectuals accounts for the great amount of sheer verbalism that now floods our civilization in this age of media and communications.)

But whence do we derive these intuitions? Only from our sense perceptions, and these latter always come to us within the framework of space and time. And our thinking, in turn, can operate only within that framework, for it is bound to the materials with which it deals. It can synthesize and organize those materials, sometimes in the brilliant and quite unexpected ways of modern science, but it can never depart altogether from them.

Here is an altogether revolutionary conception of thinking and mind, if we compare it with the classical tradition of, say, Plato. The Greek, too, understands that our thinking takes off from sensory experience, that intellect is originally rooted in the sensible world; but he stresses (perhaps also for ethical reasons) that it is able to be delivered, and escape, from that world. From the welter of sensations, the mind produces a universal, an idea, and thereby ascends from the *sensible* to the *intelligible* world. If we try to picture this, we can imagine our ordinary sensory world as like a horizontal line or plane, and the origination of an idea is an arrow that shoots up and takes us with it into that higher, nonsensory world. But, for Kant, the arrow bends back parallel to the horizontal line of sensory experience, for that is the region in which it has to do its work and in connection with which it has its meaning. Thinking does not take us into an intelligible world; it simply reorganizes and synthesizes this world of the senses. Thus the number system, as we have already seen, is a human construct, a product of the human mind; but this construct does not lead us out of this world, for numbers and numbering are one of the prime means by which we organize this sensory world of ours.

Thus Kant's view of the mind could be called essentially

pragmatic, and in this respect he is the father of later pragmatism. The mind has a practical function in creating new ways to organize our experience. And if we put this together with the long passage about the origin of modern science that we previously cited, we can say that mind (or mind in this use) is essentially pointed toward technology. For the requirement that its thinking always be accompanied by some mental picture implies the possibility that those pictures somewhere along the line may be transformed into mechanical designs. And from an evolutionary point of view we might say that mind (in its conceptual and scientific use) is an extension of our sensory faculties. For it functions to correct and extend these. It helps us to see our way farther and better in going about our ordinary world.

But this is not the whole story of mind, as we shall see in a moment. There is another domain of mind, into which it is inevitably drawn, and where the conceptual intellect cannot help it.

God

For the readers of Kant's own time the most sensational impact of his thought was his destruction of the proofs of the existence of God. The more pious were shocked, and they saw in this quiet little professor one more scandalous case of the revolutionary times that were brewing toward the end of the eighteenth century. At one fell blow Kant had demolished traditional rational theology, and set the existence of God in a more problematic light. If we allow a little for the aspect of momentary shock, these contemporaries were fundamentally right. Kant's criticisms of the traditional proofs were to mark a revolutionary change in Western thought and in the relation of modern man to God.

Yet it is important to observe at the outset that his criticisms here flow from his understanding of the nature of the human mind, its specific powers and limitations, and particularly of the kind of meaningful concepts our minds can form.

Let us go back to Leibnitz for a moment. His reasoning about God runs as follows. We begin with the contingent beings of the world around us. A contingent being is one that comes into and passes out of existence and is causally conditioned by other contingent beings. All that we know (through our experience of the senses and understanding) are contingent beings. Even the "everlasting hills" were begotten by geologic convulsion and are worn away by weather and time. Nature is a chain of such contingent beings, or many chains interlocking, and perhaps infinite—chain upon chain. Now we step back a little and try to form a notion of the whole, of all that is. Why do these chains exist? Why does any chain at all exist? And we come upon that awesome question that inevitably confronts the human mind when it pushes its thought far enough: Why does anything at all exist, rather than nothing?

And here Leibnitz invokes the principle of sufficient reason. This principle tells us that nothing exists without some reason, or cause, for its existence. There is nothing obscure about this principle as it functions within our experience. We use it as we go from link to link in the causal chain of nature, ever pushing farther and backward. If it works for the part, why not for the whole chain? We have, then, to go outside the chain: the sufficient reason we seek can be found only in some noncontingent, or Necessary, Being. And Necessary Being is what the tradition of religious worship invokes and prays to as God.

So far, Leibnitz is speaking for the whole tradition of rational theology. Kant's refutation is short and sharp, but it in fact requires the whole of his *Critique of Pure Reason*, with its doctrine of mind, to give it teeth.

The mistake of Leibnitz, says Kant, is to extend illegitimately the principle of sufficient reason, or causality, beyond the sphere of our possible experience. The principle does indeed function clearly within the framework of our ordinary experience; indeed, it is the framework within which our experiences find their structure and function. But precisely because it is part of that framework, it cannot be invoked beyond it. We are creatures of space and time, and the power of our mind (the glory of our science) is to synthesize the things that are found within space and time, and have meaning only within that framework. When we seek to go beyond that framework, our concepts are no longer clear-cut enough to admit of proof or disproof. We are in a transcendent realm where other human attitudes come into play, but not the possibility of definite proof or disproof.

Thus Kant even raises the question whether the concept of a Necessary Being itself is really definite and meaningful. We can, of course, provide a kind of verbal definition of such a being. We know what a contingent being is, and we may then simply define a Necessary Being as one that is noncontingent. But does such a verbal formula suffice to give any definite *content* to the idea? Are we merely talking about words? The verbal formula, which comes so pat, does not provide us any way to construct the definite content—the intuitions by which we would bring it before the mind—of this idea. It remains, therefore, merely a verbal formula without strict content.

Kant's point is fundamental here, and we may notice that it has resurfaced again in contemporary debates on the foundations of mathematics. Is a mathematical set sufficiently determinate when we have given a merely verbal description of it— a description, however, that leaves us no way to construct it? Is it not, then, empty of mathematical content? The debate on the foundations of set theory turns on this question. Kant and his modern followers are here more rigorous in their requirements for meaning than, say, Bertrand Russell, who accepts mathematical entities that are defined by verbal formulae the words of which are generally understandable but provide no method of construction.

But to come back to theology and the Necessary Being. When Kant says this idea has no positive and definite content, he is not saying—in the style of positivism—that it is "meaningless" and should be discarded. His thought provides material for the positivists, but he is far from following their uncritical negativism. This is why his philosophy is a great historical fork in the road from which modern positivism takes one road —but it is not Kant's road. When he says the idea of a Necessary Being does not have definite content, he does not mean to say it is "meaningless," but only that it is not a clear-cut concept, like those of science, about which proof and disproof are possible. Here Kant introduces his distinction between ideas and concepts. The idea of God is not meaningless, because it can never become like a strict concept in science; it belongs to another order of mind and lays claim upon other portions of our being. Indeed, as human beings, we exist within the question of God, and we can never quite escape it, however we turn our backs upon it.

In the matter of the proofs of God, then, who is right, Leibnitz or Kant, the theological tradition or modern criticism? On one very plain practical ground, Kant would certainly seem to be right: *De facto* there is no proof of the existence of God. If there were, there would be far fewer unbelievers walking around today. We are using proof here in the strict sense as that which, when clearly and distinctly established, compels the assent of all. Sometimes in mathematics there are questionable proofs that hang around for quite a while before their fate is determined. And this is certainly the case in the contentions of modern mathematicians about the foundations of their subject. And in those questionable cases decision will come only when constructive proofs (such as Kant would have required) are established. Proof is proof; and when a really satisfactory proof is given, the matter has been settled. Nothing like this has happened for proofs in the theological domain. Otherwise the whole direction of our present civilization would be different.

Yet Leibnitz's thought here cannot be brushed aside as an idle fallacy. His reasoning places our intellect against the question it cannot evade: Why is there anything at all, rather than nothing? We may speak of the need of faith here, but simply as intellectual beings we are brought to confront this question. It gapes before us. If our civilization were to continue a thousand years and science were to make continuous progress in ways unimaginable to us now, humankind would still face this question, and on the same terms as we confront it today. Kant's refutation at least performs this service for the religious: It tells them that science can never answer this question that we are supremely concerned with as human beings. Science can never take the place of religion: perform its functions or answer its questions.

Here the intellect brings us before a question with which, in terms of exact reasoning, it cannot cope. This is its radical finitude. We usually think of finitude in the form of a line that has to be terminated somewhere: it goes on so far and no farther, but there is always the beckoning beyond, where we might—who knows?—find what we want. But here the finitude is at the very beginning of the process. It is as if there were a great, gaping hole at the center of our reason. This reason of ours is not of a *kind* to answer the question that it brings before us.

While writing these lines, I have been watching a spider establish itself and its web in a corner of the window outside. For several days, as the web slowly develops, it has been a companion in my meditation so that I feel almost a sense of intimacy with the creature. What kind of mind does the spider have? What is its consciousness like? It seems so neatly contained in its little world. How remote to it, how impossible for it to grasp, are these reflections of mine that are going on in me just a few feet from it, on the other side of the window? For the moment it has become for me a symbol of the finitude of our human mind. We humans are farther along the scale of evolution, perhaps, but in our own way we are as finite and our mind as attached to its own conditions as the spider's to its own. We spin the brilliant web of our scientific concepts, but we cannot step beyond it.

Yet we cannot but exist in the questions that would take us beyond our powers. One of the mistakes of students of Kant, as I've observed them over the years, is to take the three areas of mind he examines as relatively external or added to each other. *The Critique of Pure Reason* is divided into three parts: the examination (1) of sensibility (our powers of sense perception), (2) of understanding (the conceptual or scientific intellect), and (3) of reason (the part of the mind that deals with transcendent ideas). The student struggles dutifully through one part, goes on to the second, then the third. He adds one block to the next. The picture is something like a house with three stories, each floor added on top of the next lower, but external to it:

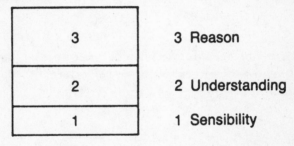

3	3 Reason
2	2 Understanding
1	1 Sensibility

But this is not the picture Kant would have us see. The later phases are not added externally to the earlier. The categories of the understanding, for example, are not added to sensibility, which supposedly is self-sufficient in its own right. On the contrary, as the framework within which our senses operate, these categories function integrally within our sense experience. Take, for example, the categories of substance and causality. When I look around the room now, I see chairs, table, sofa, etc. I do not see floating impressions or sense data, à la Hume, to which I then paste on the concept of substance. The latter concept is, in fact, analyzed out of that concrete whole that is my perception of the room. Similarly with cause and effect. On the street we see one car sideswipe another and spin it around. We have witnessed cause and effect, not two successive events to which we then pin on the notions of cause and effect.

We need, then, a different picture of what Kant is after. Not successive floors added one to another, and each external to the other, but concentric circles, the larger enclosing the smaller:

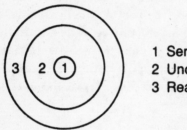

1 Sensibility
2 Understanding
3 Reason

But this is not enough. We have to indicate that the larger area of mind—the larger circle—is not external to the lesser, but penetrates it through and through. Thus:

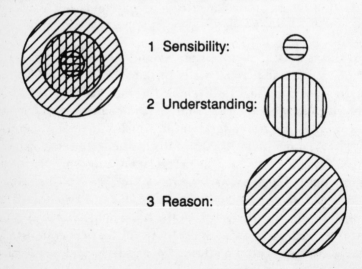

1 Sensibility:

2 Understanding:

3 Reason:

Consider now the widest circle—that part of mind that is concerned with transcendent ideas like God. The intent of the diagram is to represent this circle as penetrating the inner circle of sense perception. Does this mean that we, like the poor savage in Pope's *Essay on Man*, see God in clouds and hear Him in the wind? Perhaps in exceptional visionary cases. But we are not concerned here with such rarities. Our concern is with our day-to-day, mundane experience in this life. How, then, is the transcendent always present, or possibly present, within that world? Simply because whatever we take in in our ordinary perception is part of a larger context and ultimately of the totality of all that is. The context is always present, even though with many people it may hover for the most part in the background and never be provoked into the forefront of consciousness. But even as hovering presence, it is part of our experience now.

We exist within the totality of all that is. Is it enough for us, however, as struggling humans, merely to brood over this matter like lyrical poets, in the fashion of Heidegger? As moral beings, we are thrown into the question, Why? Why this world? Why is there anything at all, rather than nothing? And we clamor for an answer that, alas, the poor intellect can never settle. For Heidegger, the essence of our human being is that we exist within Being. But, following Kant, we would go farther: We exist within the question of God. We cannot escape it; it is always there for us, however we may seek to forget or evade it.

Nor are we pushed into this transcendent realm merely as a matter of speculative questioning. Some of our more ordinary emotions really push us there, or already inhabit that region, although unbeknownst to the person who feels them. Consider that dull, wordless feeling that can gnaw at any of us and which we sometimes translate into the question, What is the meaning of my life? And perhaps further, What is the meaning of life? The mood, when it strikes us, cannot be answered on the level of empirical facts and clear-cut concepts—the level of understanding, as Kant calls it. For example, suppose I am in the grip of this malaise and to seek an answer I fetch a look at my dossier. Well then, I have accomplished this and that, I am not exactly nobody. As for the rest, I must accept stoically my limits. Then I turn to personal and human relations: I have friends and wife and children to be proud of, etc., etc. But these factual items of reassurement do not assuage the pain of my question. The question comes from elsewhere.

It is not at all a question of factual achievement. Fame and fortune do not provide a resolution. The greatest of humankind may be put on the rack of this question. The classic case perhaps is Tolstoi's *My Confession*, one of the most powerful human documents on this struggle with meaning. A great and famous author, rich, in the prime of health, with loving wife and children, Tolstoi nevertheless suddenly finds himself one day with this awful incertitude. Why? What for? What does it all mean? And his intellect can find no answer; it cannot even tell him what kind of an answer he is looking for or where it would come from. Indeed, the experience we go through here is not adequately translated into the question, What is the meaning of life? which suggests a definite answer by fact and logic. This is why, when a modern analytic philosopher attempts (and only rarely so) to look at the question, the real question slips away from his grasp.[1] The feeling here, which is really the content behind the question, points beyond the world of empirical facts and clear-cut concepts.

Perhaps our feelings have a metaphysical depth beyond that of the rational intellect. Perhaps they lay hold, however dimly, of something in the cosmos inaccessible to reason. Kant, as a thoroughgoing rationalist of the Enlightenment, could never say that. Nevertheless, he recognized that there are other ways toward God besides the speculative intellect. Our experiences as moral agents, and as beings sensitive to the beauty of nature, point that way.

[1] As recently with Professor Robert Nozick.

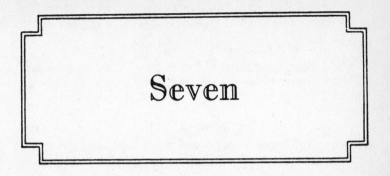

Seven

Duty and Beauty

The Command of Duty

WE HAVE SPOKEN of Kant as the pivot, or turning point, in the consciousness of the West. He is the first thinker in whom the full significance of the scientific revolution has come to be grasped, as well as its consequences for religious thought generally. We could equally well speak of him as a fork in the road of our Western history. Now, a fork is a split in the road, the point where the original road divides in two. But this particular fork is not a split in a road external to us. On the contrary, it is a split within the human mind itself. It marks a division within our human nature between its scientific and religious interests; the philosopher is now left with the delicate task of trying to heal the breach.

That the split is one within human nature itself Kant makes clear in one of his most famous passages, which even those who know very little of this philosopher may recall:

> Two things fill the mind with ever new and increasing admiration and awe, the oftener and more steadily we reflect upon them: the starry heavens above me and the moral law within me.

And he goes on to draw the contrast between these two realities—outer and inner, natural and moral—in the starkest possible terms; indeed, more starkly than any philosopher before him.

The starry heavens open before me the vista of a cosmos that broadens out into the unbounded expanse of world beyond world, system beyond system. In confrontation with that immensity, my own personal significance is diminished. Facing this universe, I am but an infinitesimal speck of matter that must in the end give back to the universe those bits of matter I have borrowed for a while.

On the other hand, if I turn inward to the sense of the moral law that grips my conscience, my dignity as a human person appears exalted. As a spiritual being, I seem no longer to be merely a tiny speck of matter in an indifferent universe. The moral law that commands me inwardly seems to open upon a fuller destiny than that.

The difference between these two perspectives seems irreconcilable. And as we yield to one or the other perspective, our human nature is radically split. Kant's formulation of this human condition is more philosophically explicit and articulate, but at bottom it is the same sense of alienation that haunts Pascal when he records the sense of emptiness and desolation before a universe that knows us not: "The eternal silence of those infinite spaces frightens me." It is the same alienation that runs through the whole of modern culture, however we may disguise it under forms of social protest. And ultimately this alienation will be healed only if the universe is believed to have some meaning in harmony with our own spiritual and moral aims—which means, in effect, the discovery or rediscovery of God.

Kant will follow the theistic tradition here, but in the nontraditional way of his own new critical philosophy. But before we trace him on that rather tortuous course, let us pause one further moment to reflect on the extraordinary thing that has happened here: the separation of the natural and the moral, the cleft between man as a moral agent and nonmoral universe of which he is an offspring.

Ancient thinkers did not feel this way on the subject of human ethics. For them there was no severance of the natural and the moral. In Aristotle's ethics, for example, morality is the fulfillment of human nature; virtue means excellence. And just as our physical virtue, or excellence, is the perfection of our bodily capacities, our intellectual virtues the fulfillment of our natural capacities of mind, so our moral virtues are the perfection of our social nature as citizens within a community. (And Aristotle, gazing at the stars in his Mediterranean world, carried away another impression than Kant from the cold gray skies of his Königsberg: the southern stars, ablaze with light and life, suggested another ethereal habitat for spirit.) Nor did medieval Christianity fundamentally alter this picture. The universe was the creation of a loving God and thus a congenial habitat for our moral nature. If the medievals added the supernatural, or theological, virtues to the schema of Aristotle, these virtues, too, are planted in our human nature. We are so created that our hearts naturally long for God, and we are restless until we rest in Him.

But now, suddenly, this harmony between the cosmic and the human has vanished. Suddenly—for it was the work of a few short centuries, which is a brief time in the long stretch of human history—modern science, on the scene by the early-seventeenth century, has come to put another image of the cosmos before our imagination: a picture of the universe as a vast and impersonal machine indifferent to our human purposes. And just as Kant had been the first philosopher to grasp the scientific and intellectual significance of modern science as method and concept, now he must go on to articulate its human consequences in morals and aesthetics.

Not that, even in our very ordinary experience, we do not find reason to doubt that the natural and the moral are always happily conjoined. Too often, the struggle to be moral in a given situation is a painful chore that goes against the grain of our natural inclination. Our childhood was a tale of tears at the struggle to comply with the commands of parents and elders. And yet, how much worse off we should have been without those tears and those commands. The permissiveness of recent years has left us with a crop of ruined youth who now lament the indulgence of their parents.

But if we learn morality through example and instruction, it would be a mistake to think we can define the moral in terms of any kind of social conditioning. Kant's ethics, indeed, is one of the most sharply drawn of nonnaturalistic theories. The fundamental ethical notions cannot be defined by any set of natural predicates—that is, in terms of physical, social, psychological, or psychoanalytical conditions. However thorough our social conditioning, we can always rise to question it and in some cases reject it. In the history of humankind there are the serious moral rebels who have experienced the call of conscience against the heavy weight of custom and tradition— and however much we may respect these latter, in some cases we have had in the end to yield morally to the voices of rebellion.

The fundamental situation in ethics is that of the individual asking himself: "What *ought* I to do?" This "ought" can never be defined in terms of an *is*—that is, in terms of any fact or set of facts. The factual, what *is* the case, and the ethical, what *ought to be*, are two very different questions, even if in some unusual and happy situations the two do in fact coincide and what is actually the case is indeed the best that could be.

The human animal as the moral animal is the bearer of this

"ought"—the one creature in nature who submits to its call. How can we explain the power and weight this call of duty— the ought, the moral imperative—has over us? Kant's answer here is divided. On the one hand, it is religious and spiritual: We experience this call because, however vast and indifferent the universe that surrounds us, we are creatures who are haunted by the feeling that we have some spiritual destiny beyond the material order. To put it tersely, duty—the call of conscience—is the voice of God within us. On the other hand, Kant is a child of his age, a thoroughgoing exponent of the rationalism of the Enlightenment; and he seeks, accordingly, a purely formal or logical explanation of the moral imperative. This division of mind here is, again, a mark of division within the mind of the West: The moral and religious consciousness is on its way to being secularized by the rationalism of the new age.

His treatment of lying may serve us as an example here. There is an obligation not to lie—no doubt about that. However often the complications of our social life may drag us into telling a lie, we are still uneasy about it and dreadfully ashamed whenever we are exposed as lying, even when the lie in question is a fairly trivial one. Whence this power of the command "Thou shalt not lie!" over us? Kant tells us that the moral command is planted in the very rationality of our nature, and he writes as if lying were a formal contradiction of this rationality. But is this so? Can the mere formal nature of our reason carry the weight of this value and indeed of spiritual values generally?

Consider the most pointed case of lying: a lying promise. I tell someone that I will do something, but at the very moment I am promising I think to myself that I have no intention of doing it. This does indeed look like a formal contradiction: I say one thing, "I will do it," and I intend the opposite, "I will not do it." But perhaps we should take a closer look; since we are invited in this situation to be logical, we may as well split a hair about it.

The two statements "I will do it" and "I will not do it" are plain cases of contradictories, p and not-p. But these two contradictory statements by themselves do not give us the actual situation of the lie. In the actual situation they are but partial expressions within more complete propositional structures. Thus:

1. I say aloud, "I will do it."
2. I think to myself, "I will not do it."

Statements 1 and 2 now are not formally or logically contradictory, however questionable morally the pair of them may be.

Indeed, without appealing to such logical niceties, we should be surprised if lying were merely a case of formal contradiction in one's logic. For one thing, we could hardly account, on such a view, for the guilt one feels at being caught in a lie. I take a little bit of pride in my competence at logic, and I would experience some embarrassment at being caught publicly in a logical gaffe, but this would not compare, in degree or kind, with the guilt I feel if caught in a lie. Indeed, our guilt at lying is peculiarly potent and intimate, and hardly of a formal kind. Once, at a small party, toward the end of the evening, when conversation began to follow a more casual and personal path, I remember how the talk turned to lies and the guilt one feels at them. What was remarkable was the almost physical repulsion people confessed to about their own lies. "My lies," one lady exclaimed, "when they come back to find me, are like sticky little worms crawling over me." The lie, in short, provokes a kind of intimacy of disgust, as if one's whole person—body and soul—had been contaminated. Hardly the feeling that logical form had been violated!

To be sure, there is a kind of contradiction involved in lying, but it is certainly not of a formal kind. Language is the realm of the open, and in speaking, in using language, I would enter this open realm. But when I lie, I shut myself off from this realm of the open and from others. The gesture I make toward opening myself up to others becomes the act by which I seal myself off from them. I sever myself from the community of human souls. Hence the peculiarly drastic sense of guilt that one can sometimes experience at what might seem only a "white lie."

The sense of this community of human souls lies at the basis of our ethics. It is the a priori condition of our legitimate, nonneurotic sense of guilt: The act for which we feel guilty is one that severs us from this spiritual community. And this sense of the community of souls is at the root of our feeling of obligation or duty. In feeling that I ought to do a particular act, that indeed I am bound to do it, I take my place in this spiritual community that embraces all humanity.

Kant will later acknowledge the importance of this kingdom of souls, or ends, when he comes to deal with the religious justification of morality. But, for the moment, he proceeds as if morality could get along without it and be grounded on formal reason alone. On the contrary, the fact of duty itself requires this notion of a spiritual community. From the moment we feel that demand of a duty upon us, we enter that community. We are not alone; as moral beings we are a part of all mankind. And this condition must be acknowledged at the very outset of our theory, and not brought in afterward as a kind of religious postscript to a system that might claim otherwise to be valid in formal terms alone.

BEAUTY

The split between these two worlds in Kant, physical and moral, has, then, somehow to be healed. In our actual experience, in fact, this rift between the two worlds does often seem to be overcome. As purely sensory beings, enjoying the beauties of nature, we seem to exist beyond that grim separation of the universe of physics from the spiritual world posited by our moral demands. Our days are sometimes blessed by the beauties of sunrise and sunset, the flowerings of spring and summer, and it is easy for us in such situations to yield to the belief that there is some underlying spiritual harmony between ourselves and nature.

But wherever there is such a natural drive or tendency in us, it must, according to Kant, submit to a rational critique to determine its proper limits and validity. This is the rationalist in Kant: In the end, it must be human reason that sets up order in the household of human faculties. Otherwise these faculties would be like a garden growing wild, each impinging upon the other. Hence the last of Kant's three great critiques is given over to an examination of ourselves as sensory beings, as aesthetic perceivers.

It is important to take note of the symmetry of these three works. Kant's thought is one of the last great efforts in Western thought toward systematic wholeness. Different as it is, his work nevertheless bears a certain resemblance to the medieval summas in its search for systematic unity and completeness. Thus the *Critique of Pure Reason* deals with our human being as scientist and knower; the second, the *Critique of Practical Reason*, with the human person as moral agent. The last, the *Critique of Judgment*, brings these separate aspects together in an analysis of the human being as an aesthetic and sensory perceiver—a creature of the senses who is also a spiritual and moral agent. Thus it deals with the complete human person and has, accordingly, a kind of completeness beyond the earlier works. That is why Hegel, who comes in the next generation of philosophers and was in his own particular way a careful reader of Kant, held this last to be the greatest of the three critiques. Be that as it may, there is a very genial and fresh quality, a sense of ease about this work. Perhaps Kant by this time was both fully aware of the mark he had made and assured that his thought was in the right direction.

Writing about aesthetic matters, however, Kant is no aesthete. He remains a moralist fundamentally, who deals with the sense of beauty as a part of our total spiritual being. The term "aesthete" itself is revealing here. As we commonly apply it to certain individuals, the term carries some disparagement. An aesthete is thought of as a person who gives himself too much to the cultivation of refined sensations—to the neglect of his more prosaic ethical *duties*. The corresponding error among philosophical theorists on the subject is to concentrate on the experience of beauty exclusively in connection with works of art. And that concentration, in turn, must inevitably beget more aesthetes, for whom the notion of beauty becomes primarily an affair of delicate taste and refined sensation. Kant, on the contrary, insists that our deeper interest should be the experience of beauty *within nature*. For there our experience is surrounded by the awe, magnificence, and wonder of the cosmos. The beautiful scene in nature is not only captivating to our senses, but also uplifting: It resonates with spiritual overtones that awaken our moral sentiment. Here the aesthetic and the moral are allied.

Thus, says Kant, the man who gives himself to the beauty of nature is also likely to be a morally good man. He will not resemble the aesthete, whose response to beauty is of the senses only and who can sometimes combine his delicate sensitivity to works of art with an absence of moral sensibility in actual life. The pages of Renaissance history are strewn with such aesthetic desperadoes—connoisseurs of art who were capable of slitting a throat without a moment's afterthought. The duke in Browning's *My Last Duchess* is a good example; he has more sensitivity to works of art than to human life.

Kant's view of beauty is likely to strike some of us as unduly moralistic and therefore quaintly old-fashioned. After all, we are "moderns," who have been through the upheavals of modern art, and all the verbal jousting around that subject seems by this time to have dispensed with the beautiful as we find it in nature. For anyone whose youth was passed in the labyrinth of claims and counterclaims around the subject of modernism, it may take many years (as in the case of the present writer) to come to realize the depth and validity of the

Kantian view. What is present here (in the quarrels about modern art) is one more case of the separation of our human being from nature. Art becomes a purely human product, having little to do with the alleged beauties of nature. But this separation of man from nature was happening in the consciousness of the West long before it exploded in the modern art of this century.

Since we are touching here on matters of aesthetics, it may be worthwhile to notice briefly where this shift in aesthetic theory itself first comes very visibly to the surface. We have to warn the reader once again that we are not attempting any detailed history of philosophy here; but in dealing with one very large theme—the drama of mind in our Western civilization within the modern period—we have to note where major shifts in this drama become visible. In aesthetic theory, one large shift becomes very visible indeed immediately after Kant in the philosopher Hegel (1770–1831). We need not embroil ourselves in any lengthy summary of the Hegelian system or even of Hegelian aesthetics; it is sufficient to confine ourselves to a single point, where, for once, Hegel is quite plainspoken: the separation of the human from the natural in matters of art and beauty.

And here, indeed, Hegel speaks very categorically: He reverses Kant, and in one fell swoop he rejects from aesthetics any consideration of the natural or cosmic dimension of beauty. The beautiful in nature, he tells us, is not a proper subject for philosophical aesthetics. The philosopher must restrict himself to beauty as he finds it in acts of human expression, in works of art. Aesthetics, which has been the study of the beautiful, now becomes the philosophy of art—that is, the study of a purely human product.

It might seem merely a trivial matter to call attention to this shift. But Hegel, be it noticed, is no narrow positivist with little taste for the broader and more cosmic dimensions of his subject. On the contrary, he is a philosopher of the most sweeping metaphysical imagination; and the fact that he of all people should call for this change in aesthetics, sealing off the human domain from nature, is a sign of how strongly the current is moving in this direction. Modern consciousness becomes more separated from nature even as the modern mind, through science, gains more and more power over nature. Why?

The philosopher Whitehead has spoken of "the bifurcation of nature" as a fundamental event in modern thought. What happens in this bifurcation is that experience is split into two separate domains: the immediate and qualitative, on the one hand, and on the other hand the quantitative dimensions that enter into the calculations of physics. These latter—the so-called "primary qualities"—are declared to be "really real"; the other qualities, on the contrary, are assigned a secondary and merely "subjective" reality. But these immediate qualities of perception and feeling—the red of the rose, the blue of the sky, the sigh of the breeze—make up the domain of our aesthetic intimacy with nature. It is there and nowhere else that we are aesthetically aware of the physical world. Now, however, that realm is to be shut up inside the human mind—declared a peculiarly and purely "human" affair.

Hegel's assignment of aesthetics to the purely human activity of art moves in this same direction. It is one more step toward shutting off the modern mind from nature, for enclosing the human spirit in the world of its own artifacts.

Yet the beauty of the sunset remains. And it is the beauty of the sunset, not of an event in our minds. I live outside the city but not far from it, and am sometimes visited by my urban friends. When the weather is good, we may take a walk together and are sometimes visited by a favorable sunset. Then we are in the grip of a scene that may shake even the skeptical and positivistic disposition of some of my friends. The long line of the mountain folds into the curve of the river, and there just above it, clearing the horizon, the evening star appears. If the mood is upon us, we stand rapt and exalted. We are overcome, at least for this moment, by the feeling that we and this universe may be part of some great meaning which we cannot grasp or articulate but which is almost sensibly present. The human and the natural world seem enclosed here in some ultimate harmony. Under pressure, even some of the more positivistic of my friends will confess to such a feeling— though they may insist that it is, after all, "only a feeling."

Kant is the philosopher of that feeling. He respects its cosmic dimension and would preserve it as such. At the same time, he is the *critical* philosopher, and he cannot let this feeling pass muster as a proof. Traditionally, in the so-called argument from design, the beauty and order of the world have been alleged as evidence of an intelligent designer of this world, God. But proof, for Kant, applies only where we have determinate concepts, and God transcends every fixed and limited concept. Hence, neither proof nor disproof applies to God. However compelling the feeling at these moments when we stand engulfed in the majesty and beauty of nature, that we and it are part of some great design, this feeling does not constitute any kind of proof. It remains, however, a treasured part of human experience. And it would be a pity if philosophers of the beautiful were to restrict their attention only to human artifacts, works of art.

There is thus a persistent ambiguity that runs through Kant's "modernism," if we may call it that. On the one hand, he is the revolutionary thinker who destroys the traditional arguments for God and makes us unremittingly aware of the vast and impersonal universe that seems to dwarf our stature. On the other hand, he remains persistently sensitive to those areas of experience, moral and aesthetic, that seem to point us beyond our finite station. It is not a deficiency in him as thinker that these dualities appear in his thought. On the contrary, they are a sign of his greatness, of his unflagging fidelity to the sheer variety of human experience.

Kant's aesthetics does soften that stern image of nature from which he set out: those austere starry heavens above us in which our own tiny persons seem to be swallowed up and lost. The great machine does have its more engaging aspects. The beauties of nature can charm our senses, and its more sublime aspects can lift us into moods of moral exaltation. And so we seem to be led gently as it were toward the transcendent idea of a God.

But do not think that Kant goes all the way here: that he aestheticizes the act of faith as if we could enter it easily after being seduced by the beauties of nature. Though he has written as profoundly about aesthetics as any philosopher, Kant is no "aesthete" in the pejorative sense of that word. At bottom, he is a moralist. Even the validity of our aesthetic responses rests upon the moral seriousness of our attitudes. Thus the act of faith remains for him what it always was in the religious tradition: a solemn and solitary act of commitment on the part of the individual soul as a fully moral being.

Indeed, Kant describes this act of faith with a kind of drama and severity that are rather startling, and his words here merit our careful attention. They mark a new stage in the history of faith, in which past and future attitudes of our civilization stand for one moment sharply together and opposed:

> Granted that the pure moral law inexorably binds every man as a command (not as a rule of prudence), the righteous man may say: I will that there be a God, that my existence in this world be also an existence in a pure world of the understanding outside the system of natural connections, and finally that my duration be endless. I stand by this and will not give up this belief, for this is the only case where my interest inevitably determines my judgment because I will not yield anything of this interest; I do so without any attention to sophistries, however little I may be able to answer them or oppose them with others more plausible.

"I will that there be a God!" These are fearful words of self-assertion. To be sure, Kant has surrounded them by all the conditions of piety; and the claim can be made only by the individual who has submitted himself or herself to the commands of morality. This morality would not make sense unless there were some divine order in this world and, beyond that, the possibility of immortality to round off the disorders of our mortal lives. Such might be called the argument from morality —where, however, the word "argument" has to be understood with the Kantian restrictions we have previously noted. I am not raising the question whether one accepts or rejects this reasoning. Instead, I am calling attention simply to the quality of his language and what it implies.

"I will that there be a God!" Self-assertion is one of the chief characteristics of the modern mind and indeed of the modern world. And here the language of self-assertion takes over the language of faith. I will that there be a God!—one can hardly imagine such an assertion from a St. Augustine or St. Thomas. There the language in approaching God is one of humility and hunger. Even Luther, the apostle of modern Protestantism, could not have accepted Kant's language here. As an author of a treatise on the human will, Luther would have reminded Kant that for man to will God into existence is to reverse the natural order, and, further, that any act of the human will is possible only if that will has already submitted itself to God.

Kant's statement, however, would fit in with the philosophy of the will that was soon to take over German thought in the nineteenth century. Not that he has very much in common with some of the later manifestations of this line of thought. Fundamentally, Kant is a creature of the Enlightenment, with its cool and tidy rationalism, and does not share the explosive passion, the storm and stress, of the romantics that were to follow him. That is why his language here is all the more startling, as if we were observing the advance tip of the iceberg. "I will that there be a God!" Whatever else their spiritual affiliation, these words do not seem to belong with the traditional religious language of the humble and the contrite heart. They do not bow before God so much as they assert the power of the human will to invoke Him into being.

Indeed, Kant's language here already portends the Nietzschean will to power. Everything turns on the resolute and solitary will of the individual. To be sure, we are still in the world of traditional theism and the morality fostered within that world. But we have only to take a small step forward in time and those theistic underpinnings become weakened: God recedes. Then we can imagine the Nietzschean individual expressing himself in words that parallel those of Kantian man: "I will that God *not* exist, that my existence in this world be my own and not subject or subservient to any supposedly higher being . . ." And so on, in mocking parallel to the Kantian profession of faith. Kant, in his piety, would have been horrified, and would have found this expression of the atheist's act of faith to be outrageous and demonic. Still, if one reduces faith to an act of the will in assertion of itself—if one leaves this will free and dangling before its own power, why might it not take this opposite course and opt once and for all for the death of God?

We are led thus to a final question about Kant the man and his particular quality as a religious thinker. In the field that has come by this time to be known as the philosophy of religion, Kant is irreplaceable; and any student in that field must give him careful attention. His strength, as usual with him, consists in the scrupulousness and depth of mind with which he keeps in balance the various aspects of the problem—science, morality, aesthetics—that the religious consciousness has to deal with. And he is an indispensable figure for us because he managed to hold all these factors in precarious balance before they became jangled in the confusion of the century that followed him.

But when we have said this in his favor, and it is great praise, we have also to acknowledge that he is not one of the primary religious spirits in history. He does not have the quality of a Saint Augustine or even a Pascal, to name two figures more or less at random. He is not one of those who hunger and thirst for the presence of God. The quality of his religious feeling partakes of the neat and formal style of his period. He has piety but not passion. He teaches us respect and awe for the valid forms of religion, but he does not convey the feeling or passion that must express itself in worship.

And here again, Kant belongs very much to his time. He speaks for an age that was already more secular than it realized even as it was sliding rapidly into the far more secular world to follow.

Part III

Dispersion

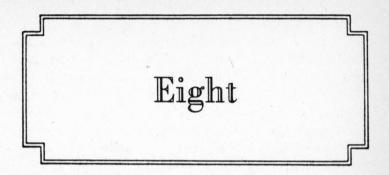

Eight

The Substantial Soul

KANT DIED IN 1804. The date continues to strike us with surprise, as if he had set foot for a moment into a century that was alien to him and withdrew. His thought belongs so much to the eighteenth century that we tend to forget how close he came to the disturbing currents that followed.

Before we descend into the maelstrom of modernity, we had best cast a very brief glance back at Kant in relation to our central theme. That theme, if the reader has not forgotten, is the fate of mind or consciousness within the modern epoch. How we interpret the human mind and its powers is central to our understanding of ourselves as human beings and our place in the cosmos. And more of modern history turns on this understanding than the more public and practical shapers of this history have realized.

What, then, has Kant contributed to our understanding of the human mind? How is our grasp of consciousness different from what it had been before him? The answer, of course, is that his achievement in the philosophy of mind is tremendous; it transforms, or should have transformed had he been understood, our whole grasp of human consciousness. We have also to ask where Kant fails us, what is lacking to his account of mind. And here his shortcoming is also in scale with his greatness. We might say, in fact, that there is a hole in the center of Kant's analysis of mind. But on this central matter nearly all subsequent thinkers will also fail us.

To begin with, the phenomenon of mind is not additive, as it was for Hume and the other empiricists. The mind is not a heap or aggregate of sense impressions. Nor is it the faded trace left by sense impressions. In fact, we have to reverse our procedure of understanding here; we do not proceed by adding part to part to get a whole; we proceed from the structural whole to part. We understand what sense impressions are only insofar as we grasp them as phenomena within the wider and more inclusive context of consciousness generally.

The example of space would be a case in point. What do we understand by space? For Hume and his empiricist brethren, this question becomes identified with the question how we get the idea of space in the first place: the question of meaning fades into the question of origin. And here again we proceed by way of addition: I get the idea of space itself, space as a whole, by adding one part to another. Thus there is the space of this room with which I am now directly acquainted; it is part of the larger space of the house, and that in turn is enclosed in the larger space of the street, and so on. I imagine the space of the solar system as enclosing all these lesser spaces, and the solar system in turn is only a tiny fragment within the space of the galaxy and the universe. Thus I arrive at the idea of space as a whole, space itself, by stitching together the tiny scraps of smaller spaces.

But in fact this procedure cannot get off the ground; we are caught in a circle at the very first step. We would begin with the space of this room; but the space of this room is in fact a particular part of the whole of space. The whole is already implied in the part. And so in general, whenever we try to produce a whole additively, we find that this whole is implied in each of the parts that we would assemble to make that whole.

Kant would thus be the archenemy of the atomistic and reductive habits of thought that have taken over so much of our thinking today. If we try to construct consciousness out of mental atoms—sense impressions or whatever—we shall find that these atoms always imply the more inclusive structure of mind in which they are found. We have already seen, in an earlier chapter, how ordinary sense perception implies the structures of space and time and of the various categories of the understanding. The part has meaning only within the whole. But sometimes this step from part to whole is not so immediately obvious. Consider this in the case of ethics.

We begin, if we are Kantians, with the idea of duty. Our first task is to understand the meaning of right and wrong, and then proceed to the particular things that are right or wrong, as the case may be. We proceed thus to the analyses of particular duties. But is this all? Is ethics no more than a compilation of such separate analyses, however admirably done each may be? And is our ethical task completed in such a listing of rights and wrongs? It may tell us about particular duties, but it does not tell us what our ethical Being, as a unitary phenomenon, consists in.

We have heard much in recent years, from Heidegger and his followers, about the distinction between Being and beings. The sense of this distinction, if not its explicit terminology, is already present in Kant, and Heidegger here has profited from his study of the older master. We do not get the idea of Being as an aggregate or collection of particular entities: this being, plus that being, etc., etc. As soon as we refer to any particular being *as* a being, we have already formed the idea of Being as such. And we as human beings already exist within the whole of Being. Consequently, Heidegger's analysis of human existence is an attempt to describe how, in our various moods and in the modalities of our existence, we stand in relation to Being as a whole.

With this latter-day example in mind, let us return to Kant on ethics. According to Kant, the task of the ethical philosopher is not complete unless he addresses himself to the question of our ethical Being as a whole. We are mortal creatures in a universe that in its vastness dwarfs us. Yet we continue the struggle and the toil to lead a moral existence. Does all that moral sweat and effort have a meaning? Does it make any difference to the cosmos at large, or is it merely one more item in the absurdity of our human existence? The moral person in the performance of his duty—and simply in that performance itself—has already answered that question. His conviction of the rightness of his act is also a conviction that this act does "make a difference" and that somehow it therefore "has a meaning," is part of some larger scheme of things.

"Somehow . . . a meaning"—we use here the vaguest of language to indicate the hope and the faith with which our moral efforts are suffused even though we may not be conscious of that hope and faith. What does this "meaning" imply? At the least, that the cosmos is not altogether indifferent to our moral struggles, and that there is somewhere and somehow a spiritual tendency at work in this universe of ours. Here Kant falls back on traditional language: as moral agents we enter the kingdom of ends. It is part of our ethical being that we belong to that realm simply in the confident performance of our duty.

Notice, however, that Kant does not assert this as a proof for the existence of God. He still retains his "critical" stance. He is describing what is implied in our moral actions if we but follow their implications all the way. We "postulate" the existence of God, we act as though there is a spiritual order in the universe and as though our own lives somehow enter into it.

Some critics have ascribed this step in Kant's ethics to the psychological baggage of Christian theism that, despite the formidable apparatus of his critical philosophy, he was unable to shake. But this contention misses the philosophical point. Whatever may be the truth of Kant's personal psychology, his general point here seems to me quite sound. Our beliefs about the universe do enter into our views of morality. Our ethical being is projected against some imagination of the cosmos as a whole. This is as true for the atheist as for the theist, for a Nietzsche as well as a Kant. Thus Nietzsche is right to project his atheism so boldly into his discussions of human values, for those values are shaped and colored, and deliberately so, by his atheistic convictions. What Nietzsche experienced as "the death of God" had the profoundest effect upon his moral convictions.

Some modern academic philosophers would deny all this, as they seek to construct a logically self-contained ethics. The effort is a brave one, but bound to be self-defeating. These systems deal with something less than the whole ethical being of the human animal as we know it. They present us with a human being who has never experienced the question of the existence of God and the meaning of life as ultimate questions that infect our moral existence. The cosmic dimensions of mind are pushed aside in the interests of specialization. The specialization of the modern mind is in the interests of efficiency; but this pursuit of efficiency can lead to the compartmentalization of mind and the consequent fragmentation of the human person who is caught up in such compartmentalization.

And here again Kant's philosophy of mind may serve us as a model and a warning. Just as he warns us against the effort of empiricism in the manner of Hume, to understand mind reductively and atomistically as a heap of sense data, so he would warn us against our more modern tendency toward compartmentalization and fragmentation. We do not understand mind unless we are able to grasp it as part of the total Being within which the human person exists and functions.

But if Kant is so admirable a master in these important matters of the mind, where, then, can he possibly be at fault? What is lacking in his theory?

The answer is not far afield; indeed it is so near at hand, we might almost say close underfoot, that we tend to pass it by. What is lacking in Kant is a grasp of the concrete self, of the *I* that each of us experiences as his own. His analysis is formal and transcendental but does not come to grips with the existential ego that underlies all those formal aspects.

The accusation is easily made, but we have now to proceed to give it some substance.

To be sure, Kant does acknowledge that the idea of the I, or ego, must be capable of accompanying all our thoughts. There are no floating thoughts, or impressions, that cannot be connected with some particular self. Consciousness does not just float around as consciousness; it must always be capable of being identified as the consciousness of someone. We sometimes get so absorbed in what we are thinking that we forget ourselves. We lose sight of the thinker, the self, that is there. But we come back to ourselves and find that those thoughts, after all, were our own, that they are indeed somehow connected to a self.

Kant's view here is directed against Hume and the latter's desubstantialization of consciousness. The self, in Hume, virtually disappears into sense impressions, and these latter float by as unattached phenomena. Kant wants to establish the idea of the self as essential to our understanding of consciousness. The significance of this controversy is not a mere matter of scholarship about these two philosophers of the eighteenth century, but bears upon a central tendency of modern philosophy and indeed of modern culture. For that philosophy and that culture have exhibited a fear of the idea of substance, with a consequent tendency toward desubstantialization, in all phases of its thinking. And desubstantialization here means scattering, fragmentation.

But if Kant has his eye on the right target, does he go far enough? I think not. He says only that the idea of an I, a self, must always be *capable* of accompanying (notice the accent on possibility) all our thoughts. I get lost in my thoughts and forget myself as these thoughts unroll; then I come to myself and recognize that those thoughts can now be connected with a history that is mine; they occurred to me even if unnoticed. But did that I, that concrete, personal self of mine, actually persist during that time it was unnoticed?

Here Kant, it seems to me, yields a little too much to the skepticism of Hume. He wants to confine himself to the minimal empiricist assertion: the self goes unnoticed for a certain time, say a half hour, then is noticed and conscious again; it is sufficient (from the critical empiricist's point of view) that we *can* think of the self in connection with the events of that half hour. But I think our ordinary convictions about the self demand we say more, namely, that I myself actually persisted during that half hour and that I was in fact doing the thinking.

Consider the chairs and tables in this room. I go out of the room for a half hour, and when I come back everything looks as it did. But did these chairs and this table persist during that interval of absence? Common sense and instinct say that they did. In the Kantian view, it is sufficient to say that we *can* think of them as persisting throughout that interval. Common sense is here more dogmatic than Kant, and on this matter, I prefer to side with common sense.

What I wish to present, in short, is a far more concrete and substantial view of the human self, or soul, than can be found in Kant. The soul as substance! Horrors! What a dreadful lapse back to Descartes and all his attendant errors! But perhaps we have to look farther back than that; in our time the idea of substance itself has become shaky and suspect, and we may as well go back for a moment to Aristotle for a look at it.

For Aristotle, a "primary substance" is a concrete individual object: this table, this chair, or the individual man Socrates. The characteristic of such a substance is that it is capable of separate existence: the color of an object must inhere in the object, but the object itself is capable of separate existence. The object is more substantial than its colors. When the question of the immortality of soul was central, this characteristic of substance naturally became emphasized. What was required was a substantial soul capable of surviving the dissolution of the body.

But there is another characteristic of substance that Aristotle takes note of: A substance is that which persists through change. It may have altered in the process, but it is still recognizably the same: a persisting identity through time. It is in this latter sense that I wish to stress the substantiality of the human self. We are persisting identities, both physically and mentally. However we may grow, develop, and change, we recognize the self as the same person throughout.

This fact of persisting personal identity is so large and overwhelming a part of our common experience that it is hard to understand why modern philosophy has passed it by. Philosophers have written about the self as if the greater part of our experience were spent in a lonely chamber, in solitary introspection, hunting for a fugitive and ghostly identity. In fact, however, most of us live amid friends and family, where the reality of personal identity is so bedrock a fixture of our world that we hardly even single it out for special comment. We know and are known by our intimates, and in the course of our everyday life we do not take this phenomenon of persisting identity as puzzling. Why, then, should it have been turned into so puzzling a matter by the philosophers?

In Kant's case, the puzzle comes from his epistemological doctrine. According to this Kantian doctrine, we know the appearances of things, but the thing-in-itself remains hidden from us. Of this table before me, for example, so familiar and commonplace, I know many aspects, but of the thing-in-itself, the table in and of itself, I remain ignorant. And the same state of affairs would hold for the mind as a persisting identity. We are familiar with aspects of that self—indeed there is nothing in our experience that is closer to us than our self—but of the self as a Ding-an-sich, a thing-in-itself, we have no intellectual grasp. I have no clear-cut intellectual concept of this I who I am twenty-four hours a day. Thus at the center of the self there is a hole and a mystery. Our own soul is unknown to us.

We shall be involved with this puzzle throughout the pages that follow. For the present, so far as Kant is concerned, let it suffice to say that he has here pushed the requirements of knowledge a bit too far. The cautious critical philosopher has leaned here a little too much toward the skepticism of David Hume. Consequently, there is a blurring of the epistemological and the existential: the requirements of strict knowledge, on the one hand, and the urgent claims of existence on the other. To acknowledge the reality of something, I do not need a full and complete theory of it. Otherwise most of the furniture of our daily world would have to be declared of questionable reality. Mind is real; the conscious self is real; and they are real in those aspects in which they disclose themselves to us, even if we have no ultimate or complete theory about their nature.

And after the foregoing preparation, we now take the giant step into our modern world.

Here things begin to go more rapidly; movement and countermovement follow each other at a rapid pace. We have called this section of our philosophic drama "Dispersion," and this title is no idle piece of rhetoric. Our modern civilization brings with it an immense dispersion of human energies, in the course of which many of us may find it hard to keep our own individual being from getting dispersed. True, there is much concentration in the form of specialization; but more often than not, this specialization may bring with it fragmentation and lack of communication. Specialists in one field do not understand those in a different field. And not only in different fields; sometimes those in the same field have ceased to communicate with other points of view within the same discipline. In philosophy itself, for example, it has often been noticed that philosophers of different schools hardly communicate with each other any more.

Amid all this heterogeneity and dispersion of modern life, it is difficult enough for each of us, as existing individuals, to keep our own human identity from being fragmented. But the situation is made worse when our culture itself presents no theory of a stable self; when, in fact, it advances theories to promote the opposite persuasion: namely, that this poor human self of ours is itself only a fugitive and fragmented phantom.

Following this rapidity of modern life, our exposition in this next chapter will go at a quicker pace and touch on a greater variety of influences. But I trust there will be no scattering or dispersion in our discourse, for we shall be following our single theme through all this diversity: the loss of the self in the modern world, even in the most conscious parts of our culture.

Our sequence of figures will in fact be a simple and natural one. We begin with Hegel as the continuator of Kant within the field of idealist philosophy. But Hegel, in turn, launches the revolt of the existentialist Søren Kierkegaard (1813–55), who insists that in Hegel the real and concrete self, the actually existing self, has virtually disappeared and been replaced by the much more vaporous notion of spirit. Here the issue is drawn very sharply, and one might have expected that, as existentialism developed and won followers in this century, this emphasis upon the individual self would persist and possibly even be strengthened. Alas, the opposite has come about: Within the camp of the existentialists themselves, in the figures of Sartre and Heidegger, new and ingenious theories of a fragmented self (though they do not call it that) have been concocted. And under the influence of these existentialists the push toward fragmentation has spread into the field of literary criticism and literary analysis in the movement known as "deconstructionism," which has already found anchorage in some of our university departments.

Armed with this thumbnail outline of the topics that follow, the reader may now proceed to hack his way through the jungle of modernity.

Nine

The Disappearing Self

THE NINETEENTH is a century we are still struggling to extricate ourselves from. It has thus something of the ambiguity of a parental image for us, and our grasp of it, in consequence, is still somewhat uncertain and confused. It was, for example, a century of quite overwhelming materialism and positivism, and with these doctrines the notion of mind or consciousness receives very short shrift. Yet in philosophy itself the first part of the century was to witness an almost bacchanalian celebration of consciousness in the form of German idealism, and in its principal figure, Hegel.

To be sure, Hegel and idealism are subjects that have fallen pretty much by the wayside. The dominant Anglo-American philosophy of the past fifty years, for example, hardly betrays any acquaintance at all with idealism and its contributions.

The tide simply moved away from any concern with the human subject and subjectivity. Yet there are signs here and there that we may have to pay attention to Hegel once again, if only to correct some of the ideas about history that have become dominant among our professional historians.

These historians practice what they call "social history," which aims to describe the routine external behavior of a society. As a reaction against an earlier overdose of ideology, when large and sweeping abstractions were thrown too easily about, this emphasis is perhaps understandable. But surely it goes too far in its rejection of mind when it would exclude the events of intellectual culture, the struggle for and about ideas, from the concern of the historian. We get, as it were, a kind of mindless behaviorism transposed from psychology to the field of history. And it is here that we have to recall the figure of the first and greatest philosopher of history, Hegel, who insisted that history was primarily a history of the human mind.

Only a conscious animal has a history, because it can recall the past and seek to make something significantly different for the future. Only the power of consciousness and the change it can bring delivers history from the aimless and monotonous repetition of the chronicle. In the scale of human consciousness, those primitive peoples are lowest who have not yet risen to the level of history. The Greeks spoke of man as the rational animal; following Hegel, perhaps we should speak of man as the historical animal.

The principle at issue here cuts both ways. If human consciousness is essential to history, if indeed the change and development of consciousness is what essentially constitutes history, the corollary is also true: History is essential to consciousness. Human consciousness will differ from one epoch to another. And here Hegel's boldness and originality as a philosopher come to the fore: He speaks, for example, of a *Weltgeist* and a *Zeitgeist*, a world spirit and a time spirit. And because of the sweep of his language, some readers have taken him to be lapsing here into metaphor and mythology. Not at all. He is referring to something well known to anyone who has delved even a little bit into history: that the mentality of one historical epoch may differ very much from that of another, and that as individual minds we are very much creatures of our time and its particular historical climate.

Consider the case of works of art. We do not need very much expertise in the history of art to be able to situate a given work in its approximate historical period. Somehow the individual work carries the look of its time about it. It bears all the pressures of its period, however individual and rebellious the artist may have wished to be. And perhaps the more he seeks to escape them, the more crudely his work will bear the historic marks of his period.

Art and the artist are under no special dispensation here. We are all, as conscious humans, under the pressure of time and history, and we carry the marks of these deep in our person as, conversely, the work of art brings them eloquently to the surface. Nor is this historical part of our being something that holds only for those who may be gifted with some special "historical consciousness." The ordinary man in the street and the man packed next to his neighbor on the subway belong to their epoch as much as the savant pondering on the meaning of history. The consciousness of the ordinary man today, whether he is aware of it or not, is different from that of the medieval peasant. We sometimes refer to the consciousness of this ordinary man today as undifferentiated and ahistorical. In fact, it is not. We have to think here of the individual mind as a bubble on a vast sea. It somehow retains its identity, but it is not separated from the surrounding ocean, whose waters seep through and around it, and perpetually sustain it.

Given this immersion in history, what, then, according to Hegel, becomes our human task confronting it? How does the individual self realize itself within the toils of the historic process?

Hegel's answer here is radically different from the traditional philosophic attitude usually associated with Plato and Platonism. The realization of the self is not an escape from time or the historic process; we do not realize the fullness of the self in a timeless vision that delivers us from history. On the contrary, since we are condemned in any case to be historical, we had best strive to be deliberately and consciously so. The task of human consciousness is to gather into itself all the significant strands of its history and make them fully explicit. The authentic consciousness is not one that seeks an escape from history but one that brings history to its culmination in consciousness.

Hegel called this kind of consciousness "concrete mind." Perhaps he would have been more accurate to call it "encyclopedic mind."

What Hegel does, in short, is to single out the kind of mind that particularly engages him as a professor: the mind of the *Gelehrter*, the savant, the self-consciously learned man. But the reality of consciousness transcends any of its special types. Mind or consciousness is real wherever we find it, even in its most humdrum manifestations. Indeed, it is with these more humble and ordinary facts that we may renew the contact with consciousness that a more cerebral philosophy has lost. Such, in any case, was the revolt that Kierkegaard declared against Hegel and the philosophers a little more than a century ago; and with that revolt he launched the philosophy that has come to be known as existentialism.

Unfortunately, as we shall see, by one of those ironic twists of history, certain contemporary versions of that philosophy have reversed field and become as destructive of the individual and individual consciousness as the rest of our culture.

KIERKEGAARD AND EXISTENTIALISM

Despite all the publicity that has surrounded existentialism, an adequate evaluation of Kierkegaard has hardly arrived among our philosophers. For one thing, he seems to speak with a voice that is alien to theirs. He is not a philosopher, but a religious writer—something of a prophet, perhaps a religious poet. And yet, I believe, his central message should be of the utmost significance for philosophy and philosophers. How is this seeming paradox possible?

First of all, we have to notice that there is something of a paradox inherent in the notion of "Christian philosophy" itself. In one sense, there is no such thing as Christian philosophy at all. Christian faith falls outside of philosophy—either above or below, or however you wish to situate it, but in any case beyond philosophy. The advent of this faith marked a revolutionary break with the philosophic consciousness of the pagan world.

Yet there is the fact of Christian experience, which the philosopher cannot blithely ignore. Strictly speaking, philosophy is supposed to take cognizance of all kinds of human experience even if the particular philosopher has a personal distaste for one or the other kind. In the absence of Christian belief, the philosopher may not be able to enter into all modes of Christian experience, but he must struggle to take stock of them as best he can, even if at something of a distance. Above all, he should not dogmatically deny that such experience exists. Moreover, there is one central area of human experience that, whether we be believers or not, we all share—and that is the search for personal salvation. We may understand this salvation differently, and we may not even choose to use the word itself, but the fact remains that this struggle lies at the center of the self. And here Kierkegaard may be taken as a profound and illuminating guide.

At the center of the self, then, lies a passionate self-concern. This has nothing to do with egotism, for the self-concern could be that of the saint struggling to sink his own private will in God's. The point is that at the center of the self lies a vital passion, not some inert mental stuff or amalgam of perceptions. Consider, for example, what a radical departure

Kierkegaard's is from some of the theories of mind we have encountered in this book. How different from the view of the empiricist David Hume, that mind is merely an inert aggregate or heap of sense impressions. Kierkegaard supplies the vital spark, and in the long run, as we shall see, he is more empirical, more true to experience, than the empiricists.

Kierkegaard deepens the note of subjectivity beyond these earlier thinkers. This does not mean that he adds any new epistemological doubts beyond Descartes or Hume, which serve only to relativize and weaken the stance of the ego as it confronts the world. On the contrary, he is concerned with strengthening the self in the face of the world. Or, to put it another way, he is interested in *subjectivity* as an *existential* fact and not in *subjectivism* as a problem for the theory of knowledge. The distinction here is central, and we may pause for one further moment to try to fix it in the reader's mind as clearly as we can.

Wherever there is consciousness, there is a point of view from which things are seen, and hence subjectivity of one kind or another. We cannot imagine a consciousness that is just consciousness but not the consciousness of some being or other, whether bird, bat, fish, or human. Consciousness and subjectivity are thus coextensive. This conclusion is forced upon us by an examination of consciousness itself, a purely phenomenological conclusion that seems emotionally neutral to any kind of human pathos. Thus we have not yet arrived at the concrete subjectivity that Kierkegaard is after. We have to see this consciousness in its existential situation.

There is, for example, the fact of death. The conscious subject comes into a world where people die, and he among them. He exists thus in a world where anxiety, in one form or another and in one degree or another, must be the common lot of all. How to cope with it—that becomes the personal problem of each individual self, whatever portion of fate it draws. The struggle of the self to preserve itself takes many forms of strategy, sometimes a desperate flight from itself. It might be said, paradoxically but truly, that sometimes we are never more absorbed in the self than when we are plotting desperate and devious devices of escape from that self.

On this matter Kierkegaard offers us some of the most penetrating and eloquent pages in the world's literature. I refer to his famous description of the stages of human existence: the aesthetic, the ethical, and the religious. We need not go into detail here to recapitulate the stages, or levels, of human existence; it is sufficient for our purposes to notice their general direction: from a desperate effort to escape from the self to a final surrender and commitment. The strategies of escape may be subtle and devious—we lose ourselves in sensation, pleasure, or the refinements of art and beauty; or perhaps in philosophy in its more grandiose abstractions, like the "world spirit"—but these strategies fail in the end, they collapse in despair, and we come back to the humble self that we are and that we cannot escape. We have to be who we are, however we may seek eventually to transform ourselves.

Those of us who profess to be Christian might do well here to remember that the central figure of the Christian religion is a man nailed to a cross. In one way or another, we are all nailed to the cross of ourselves. This is a stark and brutal image, I realize, to throw before American readers—readers who are likely to be saturated in pamphlets of self-help or even taking expensive courses designed to develop a new self, or new personality, that they may present to the world. I would not in the least wish to decry these impulses toward self-improvement, only to point out that they must all start from the recognition of that concrete and humble self who we are. And if these efforts toward change and self-transformation should be successful, they will also return us to a concrete self, however changed, that we shall have to learn to suffer, to abide, in turn.

We have passed here to a deeper degree of subjectivity when we deal with a self that makes decisions about itself and seeks to change itself or its way of life. At its most elementary stage, subjectivity is merely the essential accompaniment of consciousness as such, any consciousness: to be aware is to be conscious from some point of view or other. But we pass to a more concrete level of subjectivity when we deal with an actual subject who is possessed by self-concern and who makes decisions about himself and his life. Nor are these decisions merely peripheral; on the contrary, they can enter into the very substance of that person's life and make it what it is. We are here at the farthest remove from the empiricist view of David Hume, that the self is merely a passive bundle of sense impressions; an aggregate of sense impressions does not make decisions about itself. And the same point might be made against our present-day behaviorists, who would seek to treat the human self as nothing but a bundle of behavior patterns: A bundle of behavior patterns does not confront itself decisively in self-questioning and seek its change.

Surely, then, Kierkegaard would seem to have brought a new and penetrating light upon our understanding of the self, and one would have expected subsequent thinkers to have followed the leads he had thrown out. To be sure, he came to be acknowledged as one of the founding spirits in the existential mode of thought in philosophy, and existentialism became a movement that attracted much attention in recent years both here and abroad. But notoriety does not mean that appropriate notice was taken of the message of the founder. On the contrary, by one of those ironic twists with which intellectual history abounds, the dominant influence of existentialism has moved in a direction opposite to Kierkegaard: toward a disintegration of the self, which Kierkegaard struggled so energetically to hold together.

Here, perhaps, existentialism was merely carried along in that vast and powerful movement of modern society toward the disintegration of the individual. Certainly we have heard the words often enough—depersonalization, fragmentation, and the rest—from our concerned critics, so that it should come as no surprise to us that modern mass society, simply by its size and impersonality, tends to absorb and obliterate the individual. But what should surprise us is that philosophers and intellectuals construct theories which, in their intricate and sometimes fanciful ways, serve really to abet this depersonalizing process.

This is a serious charge, and we have now to offer an outline in documentation of it. We shall proceed backward, from the later and more widespread movement to the originating, or at least contributing, source in such thinkers as Sartre and Heidegger.

The "Deconstruction" of the Self

In France any intellectual cause that attains sufficient notoriety is likely to end as a literary movement. The practice has its faults; the issues can sometimes be overdramatized or otherwise distorted when they enter the literary arena. Yet, on the whole, this French habit has its values: We are more likely to see some of the human implications of a doctrine if we have turned it over to literary expression and the literary imagination.

The literary cause in France that has attracted most attention in the past two decades is the critical movement known as deconstructionism. Originally, the deconstructionists brought forth a special mode of literary criticism; but since literary criticism, if systematically carried out, entails a theory of literature, deconstructionism has become a whole philosophy in itself, though pursued usually for the destruction of philosophy. It has attracted a certain following in this country, particularly among academics who are attracted by what is recherché and fashionable.

As the name implies, deconstructionism is a method of dissecting and disassembling a literary text. In a sense, of course, all literary interpretation does such dissecting to one degree or another; but the degree, in the case of the deconstructionists, amounts to a difference in kind from all the usual forms of literary criticism. The deconstructionists claim as an intellectual predecessor Ferdinand de Saussure, founder of a science of linguistics or semiotics; and linguistic or semiotic considerations bulk large for them. Thus the poem or other literary work is to be seen first and foremost as a linguistic fact—a fact within the network of human language.

The poem is a piece of human language. Hardly news, you may say. But everything here depends on the thoroughness and completeness with which we follow through on this lead. The literary work is to be taken merely as one item in that vast network of signs that constitute our human existence. The individual work, the work in its individuality, thus becomes like a tiny atoll lost in the vastness of the ocean. The poem as we usually recognize it disappears into the network of signs into which it must be reabsorbed if we are to see it rightly. The poet also disappears; as an individual, or even as an individual aesthetic voice, he vanishes into that vast, free-floating matrix of signs. Indeed, the deconstructionists would have us give up the notion of the self altogether; we have simply to learn to "desubstantialize" our thinking. And this work of desubstantialization they see as one of the primary tasks of our culture.

The word "desubstantialization" is a significant cue here. It indicates that the deconstructionists are against the notion or category of substance. In this, of course, they are not alone; most of our literate and philosophic culture runs in the same direction. Even two very significant philosophers—Whitehead and Heidegger—otherwise so very different, are united in their suspicion or open condemnation of substance. It is as if we had all been traumatized by Descartes, and in flight from him were in pursuit of anything and everything that is insubstantial.

In the case of literary analysis, this process of desubstantialization has some curious and far-reaching effects. Certain simple lyrical poems seem to express their subjects so clearly and directly that there appears to be no question what they are about. Robert Frost's poem "Stopping by Woods on a Snowy Evening" is about what its title indicates: The poet stops by a wood to watch the snow falling. (It comes to mind now because I have just come from a somewhat similar winter scene.) But hold a moment; we must not assume so easily that the references of language are so clear and easy to spot. Indeed, for the deconstructionist, the referential aspects of language—the claim that language refers to definite things, objects, people—are not the central fact about language. More important in the case of any symbol are the multiple links it establishes with all other symbols within the whole symbolic matrix. Thus Frost's "woods" may not be woods at all in the simple sense of the plain reader. The poet speaks of them as "lovely, dark and deep," and he would linger with them if he were free, but he has "promises to keep," and he must go on with his journey. The "woods" here could be anything dark and inviting—perhaps the female genitalia, to whose seductiveness the poet would, but for various reasons cannot, yield, etc., etc. . . .

We are thus launched on an absurd travesty of an "interpretation"—not more absurd, however, than many that circulate in critical circles today. Now, a certain type of crude and doctrinaire Freudian, if we can imagine him, might insist that this sexual interpretation is at bottom *the* real and true one. The deconstructionist, however, is far more subtle—we must at least give him credit for that. He would not argue that the Fueudian interpretation is wrong as such; it is one of the countless possible views, all equally valid, that we might take of the poem. The error of the Freudian is that he "substantializes," that he thinks of one kind of interpretation as *the* meaning of the work. On the contrary, the poem "means" whatever symbolic links we can forge between it and the total network of human language. With the deconstructionist, in short, we are in a world of total relativism, where anything goes.

I do not believe this is an exaggeration on my part. The point is that if you abandon the notion of substance—that there are definite things and that language, at least in some of its uses, can and does clearly refer to them—then you begin to float in a sea of indefiniteness, where anything goes. To have meanings at all does require a certain degree of fixity—of persistent identity—in the objects of discourse.

The issue becomes more subtle—and perhaps also more significant—when one comes to the identity of the poet. If we are readers of poetry, we do not read only isolated, single poems, we read a sizable body of the poet's work, particularly if we like the poet, and his poetry means much to us. He becomes an individual and continuing voice to us, a poetic presence, a poetic identity. This poetic identity is not altogether the same as his identity as an actual person; in life the poet may have had rough edges, concerning which the poetry might leave us unsuspecting. But poet and man are not altogether unrelated; the poetic voice—the poetic identity—is after all a part of the total identity of that human being.

At a certain point in his development, for example, the poet Yeats begins to speak with a different voice—more simple, direct, and powerful. T. S. Eliot refers to the change as a "miracle of development." One suspects that this development was not altogether independent of certain changes in the life of Yeats the man: his aging and the passing of time, the death and loss of certain friends, the loss of one wild love and the finding of a more stable one, but perhaps above all the ceaseless meditation on life and its meaning.

In any case, the point is that a great deal is lost from our appreciation of poetry if we lose the sense of the poet as a continuing presence and voice in his work. If we are not always priggishly academic in our responses, then we may even experience the poet in his poem as one human soul speaking to another, to ourself. But the deconstructionists' doctrine would make any experience like this impossible, for they flatly deny the self. Language is thus cut off from its human base and becomes a free-floating system of signs. Without a reference to this human base, the self, deconstructionism becomes merely another manifestation of the nihilism that in so many guises, subtle and otherwise, pervades our culture.

From its generally intemperate and reckless tone, one might conclude that deconstructionism is just another Bohemian product of left-bank Paris, still eager after all these years to shock the bourgeoisie. On the contrary, it has drawn some quite solemn literary scholars in its wake, and it does have some serious philosophic sponsorship. Thus one of the significant figures among its leaders is the French philosopher Jacques Derrida, who is among other things a serious student of Heidegger. And here a significant question of philosophic derivation arises. What is the connection—is there one—between the philosophy of Heidegger, so solemn and earnest in tone, and this nihilistic doctrine of literature? Is it the case that in our culture even the most serious products of the human spirit harbor a nihilistic tendency? Are we that far gone into human decline?

The fact is that there is a more specific connection between the doctrine of the deconstructionists and the philosophy of Heidegger, and for our understanding of that philosophy I think it important to grasp this connection. But, for this purpose, we have, as it were, to proceed backward through the figure of Jean-Paul Sartre, remembering that it was largely through him that existentialism entered French intellectual life.

THE PATTERN
OF "DESUBSTANTIALIZATION": SARTRE

It was a unique combination of gifts that enabled Sartre to become the primary spokesman for the movement of existentialism and to provide the eloquence to project that movement to the center of the French intellectual scene. On the one hand, he was gifted with the power of philosophical imagination—a power that enabled him to paint the human condition in terms of bold contrasts.

The metaphysical situation of man, in Sartre's hands, has something melodramatic about it; and Sartre is willing to exploit melodrama to the hilt when the opportunity presents itself. And if the melodrama sometimes oversimplifies the philosophical issues, it can nevertheless also make a page of otherwise abstruse philosophy exciting.

The other part of his gift was an unusual sensitivity to the historical situation of the particular time, a sensitivity to what the French call *le moment*. For the youth of Sartre's generation the historical moment was the rise of Nazism, the Second World War, the defeat and collapse of the French bourgeois republic, the humiliating years of occupation by the Nazis, and finally the resurgence through the French Resistance. Here was a sequence of actual historical events that, to an imagination like Sartre's, had the unity of a philosophical drama. And the central theme of this drama, the loss and the retrieval of human liberty, was to become the central theme of his whole philosophy. Indeed, liberty is taken by him as the central or defining fact of the human condition: we cannot evade it, cannot escape it; we are condemned to be free. Since Sartre says so many other things that are unflattering about us, it is well to remember at least this thing in his favor: that he does make liberty a central fact of human being.

In all of this, Sartre speaks, or seems to speak, for the power of mind or consciousness—he is a nonmaterialist. He would therefore seem to be in line with the general position we are championing in this book. Why, then, should we be critical of him? Why take him as a member, indeed a leader, of one of the alien camps within the culture of modernity?

The answer, to sum up in anticipation of what we shall have to spell out at greater length, is that Sartre's view of human freedom is abstract and total but has no connection with the concrete self that is to be free. Indeed, Sartre has no adequate grasp or concept of this concrete self; the result is that this human liberty of ours, which he exalts as total, can also become demonic and unbalanced. It floats in the void.

We may begin by taking a passing glance at Sartre as he was involved in a particular political matter. Politics is not our main business here, but a sidelong glance at Sartre in one of his political involvements may tell us a good deal about some of the peculiar twists of his mind. Thus, this champion of metaphysical liberty never took a persistent stand against the Soviet Union; the modern evil he attacks is the Nazi Gestapo, never the Soviet secret police. His reason was that the Soviet Union is, after all, socialist, and socialism represents the positive part of mankind's future. To criticize the Soviet Union would give aid and comfort to the enemies of socialism. Without going into the parts of Sartre's reasoning here that are specifically questionable from a political point of view, we note that here he is subordinating the demand for liberty, supposed to be unconditional and absolute, to a single, overarching view of history. The unconditional turns out to be conditioned; and in this case, conditioned by an a priori conviction about the ultimate direction of history.

However we may hide from it, Sartre holds, our freedom is always total and absolute: The victim can always say no to the tyrant. To be sure, he may have to give up his life in the process, but that is a power, the ultimate and extreme power, that always lies in our hands. Sartre's is a liberty of extreme situations; the question is whether this view can do justice to the ordinary and everyday situations in which we have to exercise our liberty—always a liberty conditioned by circumstances.

It is revealing in examining a philosopher on the subject of liberty to notice the particular examples of freedom he favors. What are the individuals or types in whom he sees freedom realized? These examples may tell us more about the conditions and circumstances of liberty than his abstract and general theory actually states. The examples Sartre is attracted to are usually rebels, abnormal in one way or another. One such example, and one very close to Sartre's heart, is the condemned writer Jean Genet.

Genet seems almost prefabricated for Sartre's philosophical purposes: a thief, convict, male prostitute, collaborator with the Nazis, Genet represents for Sartre the free and deliberate choice of evil. Every way of life is a choice of the self we are to be; Genet chose for himself evil. He happened also to be a writer of genius, or we might not otherwise be interested in him at all. The discovery of his literary vocation is of a piece with the rest of his life: In prison, in solitary confinement, Genet suddenly found himself writing. The warden confiscated his paper; Genet went on writing with whatever scraps of material he could find about his prison. He had to write; he was not to be thwarted. Was this urge to write simply the result of some deep compulsion or was it a free choice of himself?

Sartre here places himself on the side of freedom. Even the yielding to a compulsion is an act of freedom: It is the choice of our self as the self that submits to that compulsion. The system is dialectically rigged so that freedom can be said to prevail in any case. But is this triumph of liberty merely verbal, or is it real?

Genet, for example, had other compulsions beside the drive toward writing. There were the compulsions toward crime and toward homosexuality. Did these enhance or diminish his freedom? The touches of depravity give a certain power of shock to the writing—at least for a while. Thereafter they begin to pall; the compulsions toward sex and crime become obsessive and narrowing. They cut off the author from certain wider ranges of human feeling and sensitivity, to which he is altogether unable to respond. Thus the choice of freedom in one direction may very well limit our being and therefore our freedom in another direction. That absolute power of freedom that Sartre celebrates so ecstatically begins to look very conditioned indeed.

It is conditioned, in the first place, by the character of the individual who is to exert that freedom. What we choose, and

how much of that choice we may be able to realize, are sometimes very different matters. We are limited by the abilities,
talents, and powers that make up our character. But at this
point Sartre takes his most radical step: He rejects the idea of
a definite or fixed self that would limit our liberty. There is no
definite human nature or fixed individual character that can
be a real bar to our freedom. We are always free to remake the
self that seems so persistently to dog our footsteps.

Lest we think this merely a bit of exuberant rhetoric on
Sartre's part, he has nailed it down as a fundamental part of
his basic philosophic doctrine. Being, he tells us, is divided
into two kinds: the being of things (being-in-itself) on the one
hand, and on the other, conscious being, or being-for-itself.
(The reader may notice here that we are back in the world of
Descartes and his dualism of mind and matter.) The being of a
thing is inert being; the thing is what it is, no more and no less.
A conscious being, on the other hand, is never just what it is;
it falls below the level of its capacity, or it reaches out beyond
its actual state in expectation. Our consciousness never quite
coincides with our being. And if this sounds paradoxical to our
ears, the paradox really comes from our own unconscious cate-
gorical mistake in thinking of the being of a conscious person
as if it were merely the being of a thing.

Thus the man who declares, "I am what I am," in refusing
to rise to the challenge of changing himself, is committing a
double error: one philosophical, the other human. He is thinking of his own human being as no more than the being of a
thing ("I am what I am"); the moral error is that he is practic-
ing bad faith: If he were really to tell the truth, he would say,
"I choose to remain as I am." But, instead, he chooses to hide
from his freedom and pretend that what is really his own free
choice is an inalterable fact of his nature.

What are we to make of all this? No doubt, Sartre is a
shrewd observer of one fact about our human condition:
namely, our desire to escape from the claims of freedom whenever we can by one excuse or another. But having granted him

this, we have to note that his whole scheme is much too tidy and symmetrical, too neatly dualistic. There are things and there are persons, and never the twain shall meet. But our ordinary experience presents us with quite different realities: When we find stability and constancy in a human person, we do not ascribe them necessarily to the inertia of a mere thing. On the contrary, the constancy of our being may in fact be a conscious project, deliberately and energetically renewed. Why should stability be taken merely as a sign of the dead hand of inertia?

Sartre wishes to eliminate a fixed or enduring self in order to increase the range of our freedom. With no such stable or enduring self to oppose us, we can remake ourselves whenever we choose to. We can be a different self tomorrow from what we are today. The promise of such total freedom sounds heady and exhilarating on first hearing; but very shortly it begins to pall and we find the idea self-defeating. How are we to go about changing ourselves if there are no persisting features of the old self to provide leverage? At the center of the Sartrian self there is only a pure potentiality, which seems at first glance to be potent and overmastering but in fact floats in the void.

What is happening here (at the heart of modernism) is no less than an attempt to reverse the whole philosophic tradition of the West. This tradition, first expressed in the luminous common sense of Aristotle, held that actuality is prior to potentiality. Because a thing is actually constituted in a certain way, it will have some definite powers or potentialities. The ax has the power to cut because it actually has a metal blade structured and sharpened in a certain way.

The Sartrian may immediately cry that we are here talking about things, and illicitly transposing the thing model to all cases of power and act. But in fact we have to deal with conscious human agents in this same straightforward way: Because they have certain definite characteristics—of intelligence, character, or whatever—we do say that certain actions are or are not possible to them. Here again, actuality has a priority in being over possibility. Unless we are counting on miracles, we do not expect a sow's ear to turn into a silk purse. Possibilities are circumscribed by the actual nature of the person.

This question of the priority of actuality over potentiality may have a scholastic ring to some readers' ears, and may therefore seem a trivial and remote matter. On the contrary, the question takes us to the heart of modernism and to the philosophy of being in which this modernism finds expression. In the modern era our human powers over nature have been greatly extended. It is only natural, then, that power and possibility should come to assume a more pronounced and dominant role in our thinking, until indeed they become dominant marks by which we would understand being itself. But on this central point the crucial figure is not Sartre, but his master Heidegger—to whom we must now turn.

HEIDEGGER AND THE DESUBSTANTIALIZATION OF BEING

That there is anything "insubstantial" about Heidegger's thought, or even that it might in any way point in such a direction, seems to be very plainly contradicted by the solemnity of his text. He writes about death, anxiety, human finitude; and what subjects are more heavy and grave than these? The question remains, however, whether in the end he leaves us something substantial to hold to.

Solemnity and seriousness, of course, can be quite different qualities, and a thinker can turn out to be solemnly frivolous without being aware of it. But here, too, we have to grant Heidegger his seriousness; indeed, he is one of the really serious thinkers of our period—a period in which triviality has almost become an occupational hazard among philosophers. His seriousness lies in the boldness and ambition of his central project, which is nothing less than to reinterpret the meaning of being in a way that is different from the whole tradition of the West. A bold venture indeed! After all these centuries, can we really expect a philosopher to come up with some radically new answer to the ancient but persistent question, What is being? That is the question we shall have to put to Heidegger. But, whatever our answer, his real significance may lie elsewhere: namely, that he gives us the meaning of being that is at work in a large part of modern culture. And that is no trivial accomplishment.

Every significant thinker, Heidegger tells us, has one central intuition that runs through all his work, and he himself is no exception. Heidegger does have a single original insight, bold but surprisingly simple, that is basic to all his thinking about being. This insight has to do with the nature of truth. And as we should expect from a thinker of Heidegger's style, it starts with the materials of the traditional view that you will find in Aristotle or St. Thomas Aquinas.

In this traditional view, truth consists in "correspondence" or "agreement": A statement is true when it agrees or corresponds with fact or reality. Thus I judge that there is a tree outside the window; I look and see that there is indeed a tree there, and my statement, accordingly, is true: It agrees with fact. Heidegger does not disagree with this simple explication of the nature of truth. Indeed, how could one? It is the meaning of truth as it figures in the humblest walks of ordinary life as well as in the more abstract and theoretical assertions of the sciences. Instead, Heidegger pushes his question into the basis, or ground, of this correspondence: How is truth possible? How is it possible that thought and its object can coincide?

And his answer here is of such direct and overwhelming simplicity that we are not likely to grasp its significance at once. Statement and thing can correspond because there is an open realm in which they can meet. If I am to match statement with thing, there must be this open space where the two can be put together. It is in this realm, or field, of the open that things show themselves, and truth comes to be.

There is nothing esoteric or "mystical" about this field of the open. On the contrary, we live and move through and within it all the time, so much so in fact that we hardly note that it is there. And yet it is the condition for anything like truth coming about. And therefore, with it, says Heidegger, we must take up our search for being. We do not begin our study of being with things or substances, in the ordinary and traditional way, but with something less substantial yet more pervasive: the open field or region in which such entities manifest themselves.

This is a radical proposal indeed, and there is no doubt of the originality of Heidegger's basic insight. Yet it often happens with a philosopher who has had an original perception that he rides it too intensely and exclusively, while shutting off other and more usual points of view. You can go through the history of philosophy and tick off the philosophers who became blinded by the brilliance of their own original insight. And this, I think, is what happened to Heidegger: We do not need an either-or here—either the tradition or his insubstantial approach—but a both-and. His insight should be added to the tradition and not seek to replace it. Otherwise we get a philosophy that tends to become insubstantial and vaporous.

Consider, for example, his treatment of human being in his greatest work, *Being and Time.* The analysis proceeds by exhibiting the various modes of our being—that is, the ways in which we are in the world. In each of our moods the world is disclosed to us in a certain way, and the way of its disclosure is that particular mode of our being. But then we ask the question: *Who* is the being who is undergoing all these various modes of being? (Or, in more traditional language: Who is the subject, the I, that underlies or persists through all these varying modes of our being?) And here Heidegger evades us.

Not that he does not have an answer, but his answer is evasive because it merely turns the question back upon itself in an endless circle. The "I" here is not to be understood as a subject, but, in Heidegger's expression, as *Ichsein* (I-being), just another mode of being, another way in which we are, along with the others. We are nothing but an aggregate of modes of being, and any organizing or unifying center we profess to find there is something we ourselves have forged or contrived.

Thus there is a gaping hole at the center of our human being—at least as Heidegger describes this being. Consequently, we have in the end to acknowledge a certain desolate and empty quality about his thought, however we may admire the originality and novelty of its construction. Much has been made of the criticism that he lacks an ethics, and that his picture of man is without any significant ethical or moral traits. But how could this be otherwise? How could a being without a center be really ethical?

All of this is not meant to dismiss Heidegger. Indeed, he cannot be dismissed; that desolate and empty picture of being he gives us may be just the sense of being that is at work in our whole culture, and we are in his debt for having brought it to the surface. To get beyond him we shall have to live through that sense of being in order to reach the other side.

And now we make a quick jump to another quarter of the intellectual compass, to a mode of philosophy quite different from what we have been looking at in this present chapter. In a time of "dispersion," as we have labeled it, we should expect that there will be diverging schools of thought, and that is certainly the case in our century. What has frequently been complained of, however, is that amid the divergence of the rival schools there seems little effort to communicate with one another. We shall have to make our own modest effort to do that for them.

Presently, the two chief schools in philosophy are the phenomenologists (whom we have touched on in the present

chapter) and the analytic philosophers (to whom we next proceed). As the name would imply, analytic philosophy centers
upon "analysis," and particularly something it calls "logical
analysis." We should expect, then, that the subject of logic
would play a key role in the analysts' thinking, though the
various analysts may sometimes come at it from differing an-
gles. Now, without the development of modern mathematical
logic, the computer would not have attained its present formidable capacities. There is thus something of a common ground
between the thinking of the analytic philosophers and the theorists of the computer. We shall try to explore what it is. Here,
we reassure the reader, though we may have to touch on some
technical issues, we shall try to keep the technicalities to a
minimum, touching only upon their general significance. For
we are engaged here, as we have been throughout, with the
same single theme: the search for the self.

And, alas, I am afraid that we shall have to come to the
same conclusion as earlier: namely, that in the theoretical part
of our culture, mind and self have become pretty much disap-
pearing items.

Ten

Analytic Philosophy
and the Computer

WHEN BERTRAND RUSSELL AND G. E. MOORE began philosophizing in the early years of this century, they had no intention of launching what was later to be known, particularly in America, as "analytic philosophy." They were, in fact, metaphysicians of a sort, advancing the position of realism against the idealism that was still regnant in British academic circles. Yet what caught one's attention in this new style of philosophy was its use of a lucid and powerful dialectic, ready to grind down an opposing position, so that logical analysis and argument came to be taken as the chief business of philosophy. Yet the metaphysics lingered on in the background, sometimes in the form of a distinct and bold Platonism.

But what really tilted the emphasis most in the logical direction was Russell's own absorption in the study of mathematical logic. This interest was to climax in 1910 with the publication of *Principia Mathematica*, coauthored by Russell and A. N. Whitehead, a bold and monumental work that attempted nothing less than to exhibit the whole of mathematics as a part of logic. The effect of this blockbuster of a work on the philosophic fraternity was ambiguous, to say the least. On the one hand, the effect was one of awe and intimidation: The claims of this work, and the scope of its performance, seemed almost too much to be handled by the ordinary philosopher. On the other hand, the response was one of indifference: Since philosophers had gotten along this far without this new weapon of mathematical logic, perhaps they might just as well stumble along in their old ways without it.

Yet the net effect, all told, was greatly to strengthen the role and significance given to logic within the philosophy curriculum. Here it is worth noting, by the way, that the place of philosophy within the modern world is within the university; the profession of philosophy is to be a teacher of philosophy. Now, it so happens that the young man or woman who is drawn into philosophy may be attracted at first by the imaginative sweep of the classical systems. Sometimes this initial enthusiasm may fade under the routine pressures of classroom teaching. The students have to be given something hard and fast to hold on to, and logic seems to fill the bill. The result is that in a good many departments of philosophy the courses in logic tend to become the main staple, the bread-and-butter course that keeps the department going. The whole effect of this process is to produce a kind of *de facto* positivism as the dominant atmosphere within academic philosophy. The philosopher—that is, the instructor in philosophy—is reassured that in logic he has something to pass on to his students that is just as exact and well grounded as anything they will get in the sciences.

What happens to mind or consciousness—those matters we

are concerned with here—in all of this? Now, there is no intrinsic reason why the exposure to logic should dull one's
awareness of consciousness and human subjectivity. After all,
it is an objective fact that there are human subjects within the
world, and some of these subjects may harbor a considerable
and persistent degree of inwardness. Yet the actual effect of
the emphasis on logic within the fold of analytic philosophy
has been to produce a decided insensitivity to the human subject.

As an illustration, we may take a brief and passing glance at
an early work within the analytic mode, the *Principia Ethica*,
of G. E. Moore, whose title deliberately echoes Russell's
Principia. Moore's is an elegant and unusual work, precious
and precise in style, and offering no great strain on something
that ordinary people call the moral conscience. It was natural
that Moore should become the favorite ethical philosopher of
the Bloomsbury circle, which had already formed at this time
in London. Bloomsbury was a group of young intellectuals
whose friendships had been formed at Cambridge but had now
continued on into the life of London. They included some of
the more brilliant young minds who were destined to become
famous, like J. M. Keynes, the economist, and Lytton
Strachey, the biographer, as well as other figures who were to
become notable in the world of publishing and editing. But,
above all, Bloomsbury expressed the spirit of Edwardian England in the years before the First World War, particularly in
its revolt against the Victorianism of the previous generation.
These young and liberated minds professed a loyalty to something they called "civilization" against the moral cramp of the
Victorians.

Thus, Moore lay ready to hand as their mentor on the subject of ethics. His approach was certainly "civilized," in the
sense that Bloomsbury placed on this word. He began, for
example, with a detailed logical examination of the term
"good," from which he concluded that the good could not be
any "natural" property. You could not, for example, say the

good was pleasure, because one could always ask meaningfully, "Is pleasure good?" Hence, one was delivered from the vulgarity of any "naturalistic" ethics. There was something heady and exciting for the young intellectual in being told, "The good is a unique, unanalyzable, non-natural property"; it seemed to make the pursuit of the good an enterprise befitting the chosen few and not *hoi polloi*.

On the other hand, there was nothing in Moore's approach that would invoke the old "transcendental" ghosts of idealism. He seemed to speak with the tones of that plain, downright common sense that the English have always professed to admire. Thus, the subject of ethics is divided into two parts: There are two plain tasks that the ethical philosopher has to face. In the first part, he explicates for us the meaning of the term, good, and in the second part he is to tell us what things have this property of being good: what things, in short, constitute the good life.

And it is in this second part, when he comes to tell us what things are actually good, that Moore is apt to disappoint his readers, at least some of them. We may very well feel that the intricate logical apparatus has labored only to bring forth a mouse. What are the ultimately good things that make up the good life? Why, intelligence and the pleasures of intellect, aesthetic appreciation, conversations with intelligent friends—in short, the ideal life as imagined by a Cambridge don. The intricate dialectic, the parade of analytical objectivity, have merely served to project Moore's own personal being into the work.

Nevertheless, there are some very serious omissions from this picture of the moral life. For one thing, this is a world that seems singularly free of anxiety. Everything seems so calm and contemplative in this world of a Cambridge don. Moore's book is really a treatise in aesthetic appreciation: The good is there to be perceived and appreciated; it is never something that may have to be labored and sweated for. The good things are there, like presents on a Christmas tree.

And where are evil and temptation in this world? Without raising the specters of all seven deadly sins, we may confine ourselves to the case of envy, which is found plentifully in the academic world. Indeed, I never met more subtle and insidious cases of envy than I encountered in the years I spent among academic philosophers. Envy seems to be a disease to which intellectuals are particularly liable, perhaps through the very intensity of mind that their rivalry generates. Moore, we are told, was a very "pure" mind; at any rate, so far as his text is concerned, he seems not to have known any temptations at all. Still, he should have had some imagination for the existence of evil, and been a little more observant of its presence in the world around him. Cambridge before the First World War may have been a serene and innocent world, but still it is unlikely that it could have been altogether without the backbiting that seems to be the lot of academic life.

A world without evil is not the moral world as we know it. The ethical subject, the real ethical subject, is the person who is tempted, sometimes fails, sometimes achieves; but in any case the good life is never purely a matter of contemplation and enjoyment, as Moore pictures it for us. To borrow the terms of Kierkegaard, Moore's whole analysis reaches only the aesthetic, not the ethical, stage of existence.

Here, then, near the very beginning of the analytic movement, was a lesson that philosophers might well have taken to heart. Dialectical acumen may very well go along with a failure to grasp the full substance of the matter at issue. Indeed, the very intricacy of his analysis may serve to conceal from the philosopher that he is really missing the point. Logical analysis and subject matter pass each other by, as it were, at a distance. This is a danger to which the analyst is particularly liable when he is dealing with a matter so concrete and enveloping as the human subject. The very terms of his analysis make that subject disappear. Recent philosophy abounds in examples.

The Advent of Wittgenstein

Ludwig Wittgenstein, a younger man, makes his entry into this Cambridge circle of Russell and Moore as a pupil and disciple. Or so it might have seemed—at first. But there was something magisterial and imposing about this young man's personality, so that he could not play a subordinate role for long. He seemed to radiate genius, or at least be accepted as a genius by those with whom he had to deal. And indeed, in very short order he was to set his own decisive stamp on the direction that logical analysis was to take in philosophy.

Wittgenstein's thought falls into two very different parts, or stages. In the first part he was the creator of the doctrine that came to be known as logical positivism and that was to have a powerful influence, even when not acknowledged, on a good many philosophers in the United States. We shall deal very briefly with it here, since it has already received plentiful treatment over the years. It is the second part of his thought that will mainly engage us, for it brings us closer to our theme and contains certain points that I do not think have been grasped even by a good many professed Wittgensteinians.

Logical positivism, as the name would imply, assigns a central and primary importance to the discipline of logic: All of mathematics reduces to logic (at this point Wittgenstein still held to this Russellian conviction). The novelty that Wittgenstein brought in was his doctrine of tautology. The propositions of logic were tautologous: They were merely so many elaborate ways of saying A is A; they say nothing about matters of fact or the world. On the other hand, there are propositions about matters of fact or the world; these are empirical propositions and are to be tested by the methods of empirical science. All human statements, then, fall into one or the other of these two dichotomous divisions: Either they are formal statements, in which case they are merely tautologous, or they are genuine statements about matters of fact, in which case they belong to one or the other of the empirical sciences.

How does philosophy fit into this general scheme? Very uncomfortably, if at all. Indeed, the chief labor of the positivist seemed to be to pare away at philosophy until it virtually disappeared. Thus metaphysics easily fell by the wayside as "nonsense"—in the strict sense that its propositions were without meaning, because they went beyond the bounds of possible experience. But metaphysics is likely to seem a remote subject except to the chosen few, and it was not till the positivists attacked the question of human values that most readers began to feel that they were hitting close to home. Thus ethics and aesthetics, in their traditional forms as systematic explorations of human values, were also to be excised from philosophy. Values, after all, were matters of feeling, and feelings are properly treated by the psychologist. The only thing left legitimately for the philosopher to do is logical analysis.

But why go on with this litany of doctrine that darkened and weighed heavily upon our youth? It is worth recalling perhaps as a sign of the real character of our civilization that a doctrine essentially so nihilistic should have found shelter and indeed flourished within the fold of our academic culture. Wittgenstein himself was protected by a zone of silence that surrounded the bleak doctrine of his positivism. He called this zone "the mystical," and it seemed to contain all the human values that a strict positivism made it logically impossible to talk about.

A very precarious balance, one would judge: to make central to one's human existence what one's philosophical doctrine forbids one to speak about. But, precarious or not, this zone of silence seems to have been enough to sustain him until he finally broke free from the positivist shackles.

WITTGENSTEIN'S REVERSAL

The change of mind and heart came through a reversal of his views of logic and mathematics. As the acceptance of the Russellian thesis of the identity of logic and mathematics had been central to his earlier positivism, so now the rejection of that thesis was to launch him on an altogether different mode of philosophizing. A dissenting critic might remark that it may be placing too much weight upon the special subject of mathematics to make it so central to one's view of the world. But, from the point of view of our particular search in this book, we have to remember that mathematics is one of the most extraordinary creations of the human mind, and how we understand mathematics may tell us a good deal about that mind. And the general reader will not be too impatient, we hope, at the little bit of the subject we must now tax him with.

Wittgenstein had come under the influence of L. E. J. Brouwer, the eminent Dutch mathematician and leader of the intuitionist, or constructivist, school of mathematicians. How far and how deep this influence went is not easy to say. Brouwer had thought through the whole body of mathematics; Wittgenstein's genius was aphoristic, perpetually circling his subject for the darting insight. On the other hand, Brouwer tended to be impatient of philosophical explication: His statement, for example, "Mathematics deals with mathematical thoughts," is much too abrupt and puzzling for the philosopher easily to swallow—especially the philosopher who has been brought up under a different philosophy of mathematics. Accordingly, what we have to say here will be largely in explication and justification of Brouwer's statement.

The main issues here can be focused on the relation of arithmetic to logic. Russell had claimed that logic could be exhibited as the "foundation" of mathematics, thus that arithmetic could be included within the body of logic. Wittgenstein now rejects this view.

On the face of it, arithmetic and logic look very different in their general outlook and procedure. Reasoning in logic proceeds by two basic rules: (1) the rule of substitution; namely, that one can always replace a symbol by an equivalent symbol; and (2), the rule known as *modus ponens*. The latter can be put in its simplest form as follows:

$$\frac{\text{If A, then B;}\quad A}{\text{Therefore, B.}}$$

What does this rule tell us? Let us try, following Wittgenstein's lead, to put the rule in ordinary language. It says something like this: Whenever two things are always found together, or one following upon the other, and you find the first, you will find the second. Logic here speaks of a world that is already constituted, and its task is to formulate the forms of discourse that are valid for that world.

The mathematician, on the other hand, does not deal with a world that is already constituted: He constructs his world. A fundamental case is the number system itself (as we discussed it in an earlier chapter), which is not found in nature but has to be constructed by the human mind. Or consider a simpler problem from elementary arithmetic: Find the prime numbers less than 100. Here we have to resort to the ancient method known as the sieve of Eratosthenes, a procedure of successive division and elimination. The method cannot be replaced by any formula from logic. It happens, however, to be entirely evident and self-validating, and does not stand in need of any "foundation." In short: arithmetic does not require a foundation, and logic cannot provide one.

Thus arithmetic resists logical axiomatization. Every axiom system that could be proposed, as Skolem has shown, will fit other systems that are not consistent at all points with our ordinary arithmetic. The net of logic is too loose to encompass exactly the peculiar uniqueness of the ordinary number system.

We come now to the more general philosophical questions as what arithmetic is, what it does for us, and what we can do with it. With Wittgenstein we have to look at mathematics ultimately from the point of view of "ordinary language." Now, this ordinary language of ours is one that opens out into the world of human action, purpose, and need: We have, in short, to deal here with the pragmatic dimension of mathematics. And here, the Russellian, or logistic, view of mathematics runs into a rather awkward set of conclusions. The multiplication table, for example, supplies us with an infinite number of propositions of the order "$91 \times 79 = 7189$." On the Russellian view these are eternally, if vacuously, true tautologies, so many different ways of saying $A = A$. But if we cut out the Platonic realm of essences, we come down to something much more mundane and functional: The so-called tautologies of the multiplication table are means of calculation. That is what they do and what they are. In the language of Wittgenstein, arithmetic is a means of improving our mathematical behavior.

But here, while agreeing with him in principle, we have to enter a serious difference with Wittgenstein. His notion of our ordinary language is much too restricted: It is persistently and consistently behavioral, we might even say behavioristic, throughout. Perhaps this is because references to simple external facts, or simple external behavior, are the clearest to grasp as examples. But there does seem to be a fear of any reference to the "mental," or anything that would come under this heading, throughout. It happens, however, if we are faithful to ordinary language, if we follow it as actually practiced, rather than legislate its content a priori, we shall find it abounding in introspective and subjective references. We do talk about our moods and feelings to other people, at least those who are patient enough to listen to us; and we may in turn discuss their emotions with them. In the vital flow of our ordinary language there is no break, no wall, between inner and outer, between the introspective and the behavioral; we easily pass from one to the other and back again. In this sense our ordinary language is incurably "mental." And so, too, our ordinary understanding of mathematics itself cannot be satisfactory without a grasp of the mental component that enters into its structure.

And here a little incident may help to make things clearer. A few years back I took up the abacus, partly as a diversion, partly as a project to see how "mechanical" I could become in the operations of ordinary arithmetic. Slowly and patiently I did make some progress: In time I was able to do certain kinds of problem quite "mechanically"—that is, without "thinking." There was a pleasure in watching one's fingers, as if of their own accord, sliding from column to column, adjusting the markers of this amazing little instrument. In Wittgenstein's language, my arithmetic was fast becoming a pure mode of behavior. Or, in the language of the computer, I was making myself into an animated robot, and quite cheerfully so, able to perform certain elementary operations without thinking.

Then, one day, I stopped to think. This dance of the fingers along the beads from column to column was not so mechanical, not so free of the mental, as I was trying to simulate. It was all controlled by a mental order, the mind-made structure of the decimal system, from units to tens to thousands, etc., an order that my fingers were obeying. At bottom, my operations, however I strove to make them mechanical, were thus a mental operation: the expression of a mind-made and mind-imposed order through the markers of the abacus. Mathematics, however you pursue it, deals with certain definite constructions of the human mind.

Had Wittgenstein grasped this point, he might have lost his fear of "the mental" generally, and his whole philosophy of "ordinary language" would have been greatly changed and enriched. He might even have helped dispel this fear of mind that haunts so many contemporary philosophers.

POETRY AND THE COMPUTER

There is no royal road to learning, the ancients said; but in our culture, now, all roads seem, in one way or another, to lead to the computer. The transition from mathematical logic to the computer is an easy and natural one. Wittgenstein's protests in his last years that mathematical logic had become a bad influence in philosophy was directed against the threat, as he saw it, that the reliance on a linguistic mechanism could replace real insight and thinking. When the logical machinery becomes embodied in an actual physical apparatus, the temptation becomes all the greater to let the machine do one's thinking for one. The question, the overwhelming question, then becomes, How far can the machine go in taking over human thought?

The tendency toward materialism is perhaps a permanent one in human nature, and within its limits a valid one. With the advent of the science of mechanics, in the seventeenth century, the materialistic inclination turns toward mechanism: the tendency to see phenomena everywhere as bits of machinery incarnate. Thus we get in La Mettrie, the eighteenth-century *philosophe*, those quaint illustrations of the human body as a system of imaginary gears, cogs, and ratchets. Man, the microcosm, is just another machine within the universal machine that is the cosmos. We smile at these illustrations as quaint and crude, but secretly we may still nourish the notion that they are after all in the right direction, though a little premature. With the advent of the computer, however, this temptation toward mechanism becomes more irresistible, for here we no longer have an obsolete machine of wheels and pulleys but one that seems able to reproduce the processes of the human mind.

Can machines think? now becomes a leading question for our time. It was first proposed in direct and explicit fashion by the British logician and computer expert Alan Turing in 1950, and it will be worthwhile to follow some of his argument here. Turing himself, in addition to his gifts as a logician, was an unusual and interesting personality. During World War II he was part of the British team of intelligence that succeeded in breaking the German code and thus freeing a good deal of Allied shipping from the menace of the U-boats. After the war he returned to Cambridge (our narrative in this chapter seems to hover about that institution) and continued his researches on logic and computer theory. But his life thereafter becomes rather beclouded and unhappy; he insisted on being an indiscreet homosexual and fell foul of the authorities. In 1954 he committed suicide, at the age of forty-one. For a man whose mind had been continuously engaged with the question of how the machine might guide and regulate life, he seems to have been sadly incapable of managing his own.

Turing's imagination leaps beyond the actual state of the computer to envisage its future possibilities. Writing in 1950, he predicted that in fifty years we would have computers with a storage capacity of 10^9 bits. Well, we are near the end of that period, and we do already have, I am told, machines that approach that figure. We are thus in a position to test some of his prophecies about the future range of the computer's operations.

Among other things, Turing claimed that a future computer could very well write poetry. I propose here to center on the case of poetry, because that would seem to be one use of the human mind that the machine could not duplicate. The creation of a poem would seem to be at the opposite end of the mental spectrum from the additive and combinatorial operations of a machine. Turing, however, imagines a machine that has actually written a poem: and to be specific, he imagines the poem is Shakespeare's sonnet "Shall I compare thee to a summer's day?" Now we must put the machine to a test.

For this purpose he devised what he called the imitation game. The question "Do machines think?" he holds to be too vague, and to give the question sense we must replace it by a more behavioral test. In the imitation game, the machine and a human being are put in a room, and nearby is an examiner, E, who can put questions and receive their answers. For a machine with a suitable storage capacity, Turing holds, the examiner in 70 percent of the cases could not judge which of the respondents was the human and which the computer, so connected and reasonable would the responses of the machine be.

Here are some of the questions that Turing puts to the machine that has just written Shakespeare's sonnet:

EXAMINER: In the first line of your sonnet, which reads, "Shall I compare thee to a summer's day," would not "a spring day" do as well or better?

WITNESS: It wouldn't scan.

EXAMINER: How about "a winter's day"? That would scan all right.

WITNESS: Yes, but nobody wants to be compared to a winter's day.

Etc., etc.

Thus, presumably, by giving such coherent and sensible answers the computer would prove that the poem to which it has given birth was not a freak accident.

Turing's argument moves seductively, but if we pause for a moment, we begin to find it very questionable. In the first place, the question at issue is whether a machine could ever write a poem, and Turing's method of handling this question is to say: let us assume that a machine has actually produced a poem. Then we proceed to test it. In short, he assumes the very point at issue. If indeed (and it is a very big if) a machine had actually produced a poem, then we should expect that it would be at a level of performance to answer very elementary questions about it. But the question at issue is the ability to produce the poem in the first place.

Then again, the questions Turing suggests are rather curious, for they omit the first and overwhelming question that would arise if a machine actually ground out Shakespeare's beautiful sonnet:

Is this an original poem of yours? If the machine is only quoting, then it is merely disgorging data already fed into it. But if the response is that the poem is indeed its own, and original, we are in for more serious trouble, for we move into the dimensions of style and history, from which poetry cannot escape.

Why have you written a poem in a style that was valid over three hundred years ago?

We have to deal with the poem not merely as a manipulation of symbols, but as an act of human consciousness within time and history.

It is a curious twist of irony that we should come back here to the same point we had to argue against the deconstructionists. For the latter, too, the poem is merely a collocation of signs or symbols to be unraveled by the literary critic from any point or in any direction his ingenuity can supply. And for the partisans of the computer the poem is simply the adding of one symbol to another. It might seem a curious irony of history that these two groups—the literati of the avant-garde and the somber partisans of the computer—should here converge toward the same attitude. But if we reflect for a moment we shall not find it so strange. We have to recall that for a long time now the labor of a good part of our culture has been reductive: the effort to undermine in one way or another the spiritual status of the human person. And when thinking becomes generally reductive, we can expect that there will be surprising convergences of differing groups. When you dig the pit deep enough, waters from opposite directions will flow down the same hole.

But once again, as in the previous chapter, we have to insist that the poem is not merely a collocation of signs or symbols. If we take poetry seriously, if the experience of poetry is really a part of our life, then we do not merely read single poems. When the poet matters to us, when he really involves us, we read the body of his work—or as much of it as we can manage. The poet himself becomes a kind of spiritual presence in our life, a personality present to us through and within the poems. But of course we have to distinguish between this sense of personality and the trivial and accidental features of "personality" that figure in gossip columns. And here the example of T. S. Eliot becomes especially relevant.

In his earlier criticism Eliot had spoken against the poet's flaunting of personality. The genuine poet, he held, is one who seeks to escape from personality—and Eliot even uses a much stronger expression: the poet seeks the "extinction" of personality in the poems. Yet there seems a rather ironic contrast between the critic's pronouncements and his actual performance as a poet. The body of Eliot's poetry, now that we have it all before us, strikes us as the work of a single personality— a unique and individual mind and sensibility. And this unity is there from beginning to end, through the changes of style and tone, through the long journey from despair into the affirmations of faith. It is always Eliot himself, a unique and individual soul, who speaks to us through and within the poems.

Now suppose that this poetry had been produced by a computer. The supposition is monstrous, but the partisans of the computer compel us to entertain it. After all, if there is one gap anywhere in the total mechanistic scheme—if there is one part of our mental life, however inconsequential it might seem to some of these partisans—then the total hypothesis of mechanism falls to the ground. Now, what would the machine have to be capable of in order to produce this particular body of poetry? It would first have to have a grasp of the contemporary state of the language, of the idiom, that would be vital and charged for modern readers of poetry. To be sure, our language is still English, and in that general sense is the same as Shakespeare's. But the language also changes from generation to generation: different words and rhythms of speech become charged for contemporary ears. Eliot, in his early poems especially, was one of the apostles of modernism, intent on writing a kind of poetry that would not be a repetition of outworn nineteenth-century idioms and styles. Then, we should have to presuppose in our imaginary computer an intuitive tact, a creative sensitivity, toward the living language. It is hard to see how one could install these qualities of mind in a machine, however vast you make its storage capacity. The writing of a poem is not merely the combination of discrete units of language.

But more than this: there is the relation of the poet to the past, to dead writers and their traditions. This fusion of past and present is one of Eliot's most original and remarkable achievements, both in his poetry and in his critical prose. One cannot, for example, grasp the full resonance of the poetry without some understanding of his critical explorations of the Elizabethans, the Metaphysical poets, and certain French poets of the end of the nineteenth century. But Eliot did not add these influences one to another, like so many discrete units; they were part of an individual sensibility seeking to define itself, and what he saw in these predecessors was something that had not quite been seen before in the same way. His appropriation of the past was also a transformation of it.

Can we imagine a computer capable of even simulating these acts of mind? Make its storage capacity as vast as you wish; we would still need to equip it with some unique historical sense, an ability to see the pastness of the past as well as its presence, and to respond to the piercing actuality of the present as well as to its evanescence. This is a sense of time and history that cannot be achieved by the addition of units of information; otherwise every encyclopedic pedant would be able to qualify as a creative historian.

Finally, to bring this tedious business to its conclusion, there is the fact of what may loosely be called the poet's development. The poet changes, ages, matures—and sometimes ripens into wisdom. He is, after all, a man of flesh and blood. That is a fact of which the partisans of the computer take too little note in their search for a mechanical substitute for the human mind. How much of our consciousness is embedded in and inseparable from this fleshly envelope that we are? Certainly it is not the poet's business to write as a disembodied spirit. He falls in love, suffers, and his body ages— sometimes into the ripeness of vision: "Bodily decrepitude is wisdom," wrote Yeats, who turned the afflictions of old age into great poetry. But a machine cannot age in this way. Properly speaking, indeed, a machine cannot mature, for it is not an organic body, growing and ripening through time. As a piece of equipment, it becomes used and defective, its wires frayed and its tubes burned out, and shortly ready for the scrap heap. That might be a metaphorical description of some human lives, but only a very nihilistic and reductive one.

So we come back, by a curious irony, to the point from which these reflections started: We are back with the disembodied consciousness of Descartes. The dreamers of the computer insist that we shall someday be able to build a machine that can take over all the operations of the human mind, and so in effect replace the human person. After all, why not? There should be no "mystic" obstacle that should impede the progress of our technology. But in the course of these visions they forget the very plain fact of the human body and its presence in and through consciousness. If that eventual machine were ever to be realized, it would be a curiously disembodied kind of consciousness, for it would be without the sensitivity, intuitions, and pathos of our human flesh and blood. And without those qualities we are less than wise, certainly less than human.

Epilogue

AND HERE PERHAPS we may bring matters conveniently to a halt. A halt, not a termination—for the questions here invoked will occupy us in a later work, as they will surely continue to beset our civilization. For the present it may suffice to take the briefest of glimpses at the ground we have traversed.

Patterns in history are often hard to discern, and sometimes they turn out to be illusory. But there is one clear pattern within modern history that seems beyond doubt, namely, the continued development of science and technology. The seventeenth century thus marks the advent of a new epoch in human history. Despite all the confusions, uncertainties, and upheavals in our political history since that time, one particular pattern remains clear-cut and definite: the continuous advance of modern science. But the sciences in question here are the physical sciences (physics and chemistry)—the sciences of matter, in short. Mind is left out of the picture. And that is why we have to go back and reflect once again on the archetypal figure of Descartes.

We began thus with what we might call the dream of Descartes. It is a strange dream, admittedly, but it is still one that haunts our modern consciousness. Descartes dreams of the universe as a single machine, but there inside it, at its center, is that miraculous thing, his own consciousness, in the light of which he sees and meditates. Modern partisans of the machine would snuff out this little candle of consciousness as unnecessary and paradoxical.

Thus one recent philosopher has characterized this vision of Descartes as the doctrine of "the ghost in the machine." The phrase is a telling one and has gained wide circulation. It is meant to stigmatize the extremity of the Cartesian vision, and its net effect has been to discourage attention to mind and consciousness and thereby serve to make them even more "ghostly" and negligible than they had been. But perhaps mind is not ghostly if we recall with Kant (see our earlier chapter) that it is the power of mind that creates the systems of mechanics that here seek to extinguish it. The advent of human consciousness in the course of evolution, far from being "ghostly," has been earthshaking in its consequences.

The particular machine with which we moderns would now replace consciousness is, of course, the computer. I have had no intention here of launching any diatribe against the computer as such, a tool that has its valuable and now indispensable uses. Our quarrel, rather, is with the fantasies of science fiction or of illicit metaphysics that have taken shape around this instrument. And more often than not, the enthusiasts of the computer are unaware that they are speaking from a particular point of view, a particular philosophy, in the light of which they see the whole phenomenon of mind. And this view of mind is not new; we have already encountered it in David

Hume and the British Empiricists. (Fundamental positions in philosophy do not change, but repeat themselves with variations—which is one more good reason for paying attention to the history of philosophy.) This is the view that the nature of our human consciousness is essentially additive and atomistic: Its function consists in combining one discrete datum, or bits of data, with others; and mind itself is but an aggregate of such data.

It is not hard to see why users of the computer should easily fall into this view. They speak, for example, of the storage capacity of a particular machine, meaning the number of discrete units of information that can be fed into it and again extracted from it by the human attendant. And this way of speech becomes congenial when they turn their talk to the human mind. But we may note here, in passing, that their disposition to see facts in a certain way is not merely one more separate datum in the list of facts but, rather, a point of view that provides the structure for the whole.

But the reality of consciousness as we actually experience it is more than a grocer's list of disparate items. Its presence is more total and engulfing, and it can move backward and forward in time. In memory, for example, my mind may be jogged at times by some isolated fact or facts from the past of which I merely take incidental notice. But there is another experience of memory more total and vital than this. Something comes back to me from the past, from long ago, but it does not remain as an isolated factual datum; I am suddenly back in the house where it happened, feeling as I once did, living in that world I once knew. Memories like this reintegrate us into the past. I look through time, and meet myself as I was; I am the same and other. The memory is the emergence into view of that enduring self that I am through time.

And if we turn our eyes in the other direction in time, toward the future, we shall also encounter a consciousness that is not, or at least *not yet*, a mere aggregate of its parts, a listing of discrete data. I have, let us say, the vision of a particular project for the future. It comes to me not as an aggregate of ready-made items, but as a whole of which I have as yet only an intuitive grasp and which I must now proceed, with much sweat and toil, to articulate in its details. If our consciousness could not be groping in this way, it would cease to be genuinely creative, and it could not then be the powerful instrument that it has been in shaping human history.

Perhaps all these questions that we have raised about mind and consciousness may seem trivial or remote matters in face of the large-scale social turmoil that now goes on all over the world. Perhaps, but then perhaps not. And in justification of our subject, we may be permitted to borrow our last word from a solemn source: Scripture warns us, "What shall it profit a man if he gain the whole world, and lose his own soul?" We can provide a secular version of this warning as follows: What shall it profit a whole civilization, or culture, if it gains knowledge and power over the material world, but loses any adequate idea of the conscious mind, the human self, at the center of all that power?

Index

WILLIAM BARRETT has had a long and distinguished career at New York University, where he served as chairman of the Department of Philosophy. He is widely known as one of the first philosophers to introduce existentialism to America. Barrett has been editor of *Partisan Review* and the literary critic for *Atlantic Monthly*. He is the author of *Irrational Man*, *The Illusion of Technique*, and *The Truants*, among other books. He is now Distinguished Professor of Philosophy at Pace University.